Uniquely Better

Amber Vanderburg

www.TotalPublishingAndMedia.com

ISBN: 978-1-63302-207-2

Table of Contents

Thank you

First, I would like to thank my Indian family. Thank you for your hospitality and kindness. Your patience, guidance, support, and friendship is treasured in my life. I cherish the memories I have with you.

Secondly, I would like to thank my American family. From so far away, your support, prayers, well wishes, and guidance are appreciated. You were just as part of this adventure as those who were with me in person. Your encouragement means the world to me.

I would also like to thank those who encouraged and supported the writing of this book. Victoria Jenson, Brian White, Erika Mae, Peter Biadasz, and my family - thank you for taking the time to read and provide feedback to make this book what it is today.

Lastly and above all, I would like to give thanks to my Lord Jesus. The reason why I am who I am today.

Prologue

This is my story in team transformation; it is a story of daring adventures; it is a story of an exciting future in the beautiful land of India; it is a story of working within multicultural teams; it is a story of remarkable athletes coming together to build something great; it is a story of how teams can establish competitive advantage, and it is the story of a hometown Okie trying her best.

I did not intend on becoming an international football coach. In fact, I was calling the sport "soccer." I probably would not have believed you if you told me I would be working with one of the largest professional sports clubs in the world. Honestly, I'd never heard of Paris Saint Germain until I got the job offer. The thought of living in a city of 20 million people or in a concrete flat with international coaches in Asia never crossed my mind. But as I looked around in 2016, this was my life.

In May of 2016, I was a former Division I track athlete. I had completed my graduate degree in Organizational Dynamics, celebrated my third year working as a Human Resources professional for the largest health care system in Northeastern Oklahoma, and was featured as one of Tulsa's "40 Under 40". While track/athletics was my sport during university, my first love was soccer. I could no longer compete in any contact sports due to a series of head injuries so I transitioned from competing in soccer to competing in track/athletics, a non-contact sport. I also began coaching at different soccer clubs and organizations around the Tulsa area.

I had made connections in the international community through my university, city, and local non-profit who would encourage me to go further than I ever imagined. At a fundraiser dinner for a chapter of the United Nations, a colleague posed the question, "Have you ever thought of putting your passions for sport, business, and the international community together in your career?"

Honestly, I didn't even think it was an option. Was it possible to use all my experience, skills, and knowledge in one place? Could all my passions lead to one single job?

As I spoke more with people in my network, I was presented with an opportunity that would forgo the life of early 2016 as I traded my office for a muddy field and my heels for a dirty pair of cleats. I altered my narrative from a business venture to a business adventure as I became the only female, only American, and only blonde football (soccer) coach for the Gameday Academy and Paris Saint Germain (PSG) Academy in Bangalore, India. The academies assigned me to coach different teams, mostly boys with a few girls, ages 6-16, across the metropolis.

Combining sport, business, youth development, and an international environment resulted in a dream job greater than I could have imagined. I could not wait to be a part of the international team of coaches to shape this generation of athletes in the second most-populated country in the world. This new adventure began in June of 2016, and as I landed in India, I discovered that I was not alone in my Okie departure as basketball superstar Kevin Durant had left Oklahoma for Steph Curry on the same day I had left Oklahoma for Indian curry.

I had been a leader in team performance in a variety of environments before India, but leading change and performance in *this* environment was a new challenge. I sought to help our teams improve performance in a way that required an altered approach, a different mindset, and a new take on team ownership than what I had experienced in the past. The challenges were vast, but the rewards were overwhelmingly worthwhile.

Elephant sanctuary in Kerala, India

Part I
Coming to India

Chapter One
First Impressions

The moment I walked out of the air-conditioned airport, I was hit with a gust of city heat and a bombardment of eager rickshaw drivers. I indicated to the drivers I had a ride then I heard a man call out my name. A tall guy in his mid-thirties emerged from the crowd. It was my new boss.

He helped with my single suitcase and backpack and we piled into his nice luxury SUV.

As we pulled into the carport of the apartment complex around 3:00 in the morning, I found people and families sleeping on the ground. We quietly went up to the second floor and I entered to find signed Paris Saint Germain jerseys hanging on the wall, Paris Saint Germain memorabilia around the office, and sports equipment littered around the space.

It was explained that the area was our workplace and then I was shown my room. I thanked him, put my suitcase down, and eagerly flopped onto the bed, anxious for rest.

I woke up the next morning to the sound of a staff meeting happening outside my door. There had been an emotional dispute with one of the French coaches. I listened to the conflict for a few minutes, taking notes of the dynamics and approach of each voice towards the confrontation. This particular conversation was extremely heated. I kept the details of the tense discussion in my mind for future confrontations that I might encounter, waited a few minutes for the mood to settle, then got up and prepared to meet the team.

After a few greetings, I got in the car with my boss. He drove me to one of the Paris Saint Germain Academy training locations to meet the players and speak with the parents. They were preparing to compete at an upcoming international tournament.

There were a LOT of people to meet including the coaching staff, the program managers and administrators, the players, the location management, and the parents. It was exciting but overwhelming. There was an extremely high expectation for what I would do for the academies. I almost immediately adopted a new name as some of the players did not know if I was a miss or a ma'am and so they called me, "MissAmberMam."

I quickly learned to adjust my accent and my style of speech and I adopted an entirely different vernacular in regard to my profession. Prior to India, I would grab my cleats and soccer ball out of the trunk of the car then run to the field for a game. Now, I grabbed my *boots* and *football* out of the *boot* of the car then ran to the *pitch* for a *match*. My vocabulary completely changed as I communicated with my newfound community which embraced the worldly definition of football.

I finished meeting the parents, players, and stakeholders then my boss took me to a new turf pitch for the Gameday Academy. He looked out onto the vacant pitch and stated plainly, "Your job is to fill this with people." This would be one of my coaching locations and my task was to help build a grassroots program in this area from scratch.

I would split my time working with more elite programs through Paris Saint Germain Academy and the grassroots programs through Gameday Academy. This was a great opportunity to grow in both capacities as a coach.

We drove back through the Bangalore traffic and I mentally prepared myself to embrace the unmoving chaotic commute which would encompass my new everyday life.

Bangalore is often referred to as "The Garden City of India" because the city hosts more than 1,200 parks. Massive hanging tree canopies lavish historic areas of Bangalore and shield the roads from the unforgiving sun which allows the "concrete jungle" to appear beautifully green. I kept my eyes glued to the window as I took in the sights, scents, and stories of every turn. Wooden food carts hosting snacks like jackfruit, biriyani, and sev puri filled the streets. Cows, loaded motorbikes, and patrons walking by in beautiful, bright-colored clothing added to the casual pandemonium. I had a sense of belonging and home. I felt at ease with the unfamiliar and confident in the unknown.

My boss was my driver on my first day, but he would not be my typical provider of transportation. We pulled into the garage at the flat and I was introduced to my driver named Gongilal, we called him "G" for short. He was included in the new dynamic of characters that would fill my Indian life. I had a driver and a cook/maid who lived downstairs in the garage area of the flat. They were among the people laying on the ground the night I first arrived. Considering the immense traffic in India, I spent a lot of time with G and he was my main Hindi teacher, classic Hindi and Punjabi music educator, and part-time bodyguard. G didn't speak a lot of English, but we found ways to communicate and built a true friendship.

I returned upstairs to the office and spoke with my colleagues. I asked a lot of questions. I learned the academies were recovering from of an international coach blow-up. The academies had a series of international coaches recently leave on less-than-favorable terms within six months of me coming - many leaving due to organizational and cultural disconnects.

I took note of the different disastrous approaches and lessons from the previous coaches from cultural ignorance, to superior attitudes towards another culture, to poor team leadership. I marveled that the current team had any trust remaining to give to yet another international coach.

I knew it would be really important to build trusting relationships with the coaches, parents, staff, and the team. I tried to calm the rightful hesitations that had been built up from other international coach mishaps. I asked questions, listened to frustrations, hesitations, and challenges.

I met new friends that taught me how to successfully live in India. They taught me how to eat with my hands, cross treacherous Bangalorean roads, and use Eastern toilets. I inundated my new hosts with a parade of questions about Indian life, Indian sports, the company, and the teams...there was so much to learn. It was a whirlwind.

During this time on the pitch, I began to focus on what I could improve immediately and intensely trained my players in physical fitness - improving our foundation. Nearly all my players noticeably increased their speed, stamina, strength, and agility during this time of focussed physical training.

In time, I would begin to see how I could best make an impact in the academies but that discovery did not happen immediately. Sometimes, people want a quick answer, but if we don't first ask the right questions then the answer we give may not be the correct solution.

So, I began by saying, "Hello!" and asking questions to understand my new relationships and environment.

Chapter Two
Sweden

My tongue was just beginning to adjust to the numbing spice of the food, my ears were still becoming accustomed to the deafening traffic noise, and my nose still strove to be senseless around the burning garbage in the streets, when I found myself returning to the Kempegowda International Airport. It had only been ten days and I was already leaving.

This time, I would not be boarding the plane alone. Thirty pre-teen boys, a team of supportive parents, two Indian coaches, and one French coach accompanied my departure.

We were on our way to play in an international tournament in Europe. Sweden's Gothia Cup in Gothenburg, Sweden is the largest and longest-running youth world cup. This tournament featured more than 1,700 teams from more than 80 different nations. The atmosphere was giddy on our flight as we sported new uniforms and football bags.

On our flight, I witnessed young players purchase items from SkyMall with their personal credit cards and I began to understand the true massive economic disparities in India. Many of these players had second and third homes in Dubai, Southern France, and the Maldives. India is as richly diverse in economy as they are richly diverse in culture. There is poverty but there is also tremendous wealth in India.

We arrived in Gothenburg, Sweden and marched in a grand parade down the streets of the main square into the stadium with thousands of other footballers from around the globe. Nigerians were playing their drums; Germans were chanting with pride, Brazilians were singing their songs while dancing to the rhythms, and Australians waved their flag with gusto. Iceland appeared and all began a slow overhead clap. A full in-the-round stage inside a massive stadium with singers, dancers, light shows, and fireworks made for an intoxicating experience—it was a full extravaganza.

As we prepared for our first day of the tournament, I mapped out the different game locations and helped with warm-ups. I guided the goalkeepers, collected player stats, and offered advice to the coaches.

The weather in Sweden was lovely; I soaked in the sun and darkened my tan on the field as the teams arrived. The Indians thought me insane for my desired ray action and I realized they were all hiding from the sun in an attempt to stay pale. The skin whitening cream I later found in the Indian market would contrast every white-girl instinct I possessed.

The first match featured our older team which resulted in a 6-0 loss. The second match featured our younger team with a 5-0 loss. The players had filled the previous weeks with extra practices and longer sessions. They had trained to perform well, but this learning experience was not pleasant. The players were frustrated and disappointed but tried to keep their spirits up.

On the second day of the tournament, our older team lost their second match 7-0 and became noticeably flustered on the pitch. Frantic ball movement led to a loss of possession and winded athletes led to a lack of positional advantage resulting in an asynchronous flow of play. It was difficult to watch.

On the upside, in the next match our younger team tied 1-1 causing a wild celebration and a temporary lift in spirits followed by a devastating 2-1 and 11-0 loss. The older team lost the following two games soundly.

Our players were talented and had trained at the top facilities with the best resources, surrounded by other determined players. Our players had been taught in concrete detail what to do and how to do it. Our players had technical skill, our players had the ability to kick a ball with power and accuracy, our players knew the positions of the pitch, our players knew the basic concepts of the plays, and our players had a foundation of athleticism to be continuously improved. What was missing?

"We didn't lose. We learned."

This is a saying that I often hear on the sidelines of a defeated team. This is a fine saying if followed up by a very important question. Without a secondary question, the statement does not stand by itself.

"What did we learn?"

As we played each game, I observed a similar trend among the players. A player would kick the ball or get involved in the play, then turn to the sidelines to wait for coach instruction. The loudest voice on the pitch was the coach. The strongest presence was the coach. While the coach did command his players well, indecisiveness and reliance on coach instruction made for a faltering dynamic. Our players had perfected the task, but they did not fully understand how it applied to the overall game.

I thought of the common training dynamic I had observed in the academies where the players would stand in a line, kick a ball, and wait for direction, stand in a line, kick a ball, wait for instruction, stand in a line, kick a ball, wait for feedback. While dictating *what* and *how* may be an efficient way to teach a specific skill, it did not seem to be the most effective in understanding and growth.

After the tournament, I sat on the plane ride to my new Indian home and thought about the moments of players looking towards the sidelines during the matches throughout the tournament. I thought about the voice of the coach on the field. I thought about the decision-making confidence of our players. I began to theorize these moments of indecisiveness, these moments of hesitation, these moments of mastery in skill and woolliness in game application could be the difference in a game where every second counts.

I had a theory which begged a thousand more questions. As I reemerged to the land of masala and chai, I began to formulate an idea which could transform our players' athletic lives, transform our academies, and transform our nascent Indian sports industry. I began to think about how we could transform our academies from lines, laps, and lectures to cultivate a foundation of creativity, meaningful collaboration, and captainship in our organization.

It may be easy to think of this scenario as just an *international* Academy in *sports* with *kids*. But consider this: how many other organizations have a similar "command-obey" dynamic that stand in a line, receive a task, and wait for direction? How many employees have a perfected task without an understanding of application to the overall game scenario?

This is not a unique circumstance, but one which is all too common. I began to think of my experiences in business, sports, and leadership, and of stories from mentors and legends. How specifically do organizations thrive?

On this plane ride, I began to think about collaborative ownership.

Coaching at Gothia Cup in Gothenburg, Sweden

Chapter Three
Start with Why

Before I could hone in my focus on collaborative owner-ship, I realized there was another point of disconnect that needed to be addressed first.

Everyone had a slightly different vision of where we were going as a team.

Some players only just wanted to play football and win games.

Some players just wanted to hang out with their mates.

Some players really wanted to be professionals.

Some players wanted to learn cool tricks to show off.

Some of my parents wanted their child to be the next David Beckham.

Some of my parents were concerned if it was a wise decision to forfeit some study time to kick a muddy football.

All had different ideas about the return on the investment. There was a disconnect of defined success. We needed to clarify what we were collaboratively working towards.

To the education-worried parents, I emphasized my personal deep value of education in preparing for the future. I partnered with the parents than resisted them. This was not a battle. We both wanted success on and off the pitch for the players.

Some parents latched on to the idea that involvement in sport was a career-building initiative and our academy was a straight-forward pipeline to the pros. For those who desired athletics as a valid career option, I sought the delicate balance of encouraging dreams and setting realistic expectations. I knew less than 1% of all student-athletes become professional athletes. We discussed the importance of sport in a variety of different avenues.

In the United States, I had coached several athletes who went on to play collegiate and elite ball. I also coached many, many others with success outside of competitive ball. Every athlete has a retirement date. I believed it was my job to prepare my players for success during and post-competitive play whether the retirement age be in a month, a year, or in 35 years.

I explained that one does not learn mathematics to win a Nobel Prize. In the same regard, one does not play sports to become a professional. There are other benefits.

We were preparing our players for success in their goals on and off the pitch. Simple. It was important to communicate the message to all parties that we were preparing our players for success in their goals on and off the pitch. We sought to encourage growth as people of character, cheered perseverance and determination in academics, and challenged and developed the talents of young athletes. We sought success on the pitch and in life.

We were a large academy, and players had the possibility to work their way up the ranks to be a highly trained and visible athlete. We also had players who would be with the academy for a few months and then decide to take those skills and play a different sport or activity. This was okay. On both ends of the spectrum, we would do our best to prepare our players for success in their goals on and off the pitch.

Our many goals in physical fitness, teamwork and communication, technical skills, tactical proficiency, captainship, and game understanding were all connected to our definition of success.

Before we could take ownership of our actions towards a vision, we needed to clarify the vision we were working towards. So, I asked my team: "What is our purpose?", "What are we working towards?"

Author Simon Sinek describes this as starting with *why*. (Sinek) *Why* determines your direction and focus. *Why* is your litmus test to detect distractions. Sinek encourages teams to define the purpose of the organization before anything else. Without a *why* there is no aim. If you don't know the target, you'll hit it every time. We had to clarify our *why*. Within our academy, we decided that we wanted to work towards player success on and off the pitch. Other academies could define their purpose differently, which was fine, but in our academies, this is what we were working toward.

Defining our *why* was my first question to the team. These questions did not lead to the end answer but the beginning of a larger question. Now that we had clearly defined success on our team, we could take strategic ownership toward our destination.

After we had established our organizational vision, we needed to determine how we were going to work towards our vision. How would we equip players for success on and off of the pitch in India? I had to understand more about India before I could best lead my team in this action step. India is different from anywhere else that I had coached and I knew that the nuances of India would add different values, opportunities, and challenges than other regions of the world.

When establishing *organizational values* in a multicultural team, it is important to understand the *geographic cultural values* of the area. Attempting to establish a high energy, fast paced organizational culture in a geographic place that values more casual laid-back lifestyles will probably not be successful. If the organizational values are contradictory to geographic values, there will likely be gridlock in the team culture. Before leading our organizational values in our academies, I sought to better understand the cultural values of my surroundings. I still had much to learn about India.

India is a diverse and culturally rich country which is impossible to accurately generalize in most regards. Little remains constant from one step to the next, resulting in a never-ending learning curve as an international resident. Sometimes, coaching at one end of town versus another felt like an entirely different experience. Coaching players from such dramatically different environments, even within the same city, really kept me on my toes. If I asked the same question five times, I would get at least seven different answers. The most common answer I received was, "This is India."

The gorgeous diversity was everywhere that we went, and I was constantly amazed. One Tuesday, my friend Turiya and I hopped in a bamboo raft and became wide-eyed as we floated through the ancient ruins of Hampi, ignoring the sign that read "Beware of crocodiles." We floated through the Kampili Kingdom that had risen up during the 200-year reign of the Vijayanagara Empire in the early 1300s. Carvings, structures, and remnants of a time-gone-by littered these ruins - a very different sight from the high-tech scenes of Bangalore a few hours away. We made it to shore and pedaled our bicycles across the ancient ruins throughout the day to look at the remains of marketplaces, temples, and massive royal elephant stables. We were awestruck at the beautiful stories told through the markings in the stones and the little temples along our path.

Turiya saw an older woman sweeping the floors inside one of the ancient temples. We call the elder women "auntie" and the elder men "uncle" to show respect. The interaction went like this:

Turiya: Namaste, Auntie.

Auntie: (blank stare)

Turiya: Hindi?

Auntie: (shakes head in the negative) Kannada?

Turiya: (shakes head in the negative) English?

Auntie: (shakes head in the negative) Tamil?

Turiya: (shakes head in the negative) Garhwali?

Auntie: (shakes head in the negative then says the name of a language I had never heard)?

The two shrugged their shoulders and went on their way. Combined, these women spoke six languages, but none correlated. Hampi is in the same state as Bangalore and we weren't a great geographic distance apart, but the diverse culture is so densely rich that these experiences weren't uncommon.

Of all the Indian differences ranging from language, cuisine, religion, politics, traditions, and culture; one value remains relatively constant throughout the regions of the country I visited—educational values.

India has an education system and a high cultural value of formal learning encouraging many to become the best, particularly in measurable STEM professions like medicine and engineering. Bangalore is the third largest city in India and is known as "The Silicon Valley of Asia" resulting in a very westernized community that places additional emphasis on technology.

I saw time and again my players of age 10 excelling in chemistry, mathematics, and microbiology with the goal of future STEM-related achievement. My players explained that in their schools, between 80-90% of final grades for primary - school students come from final exams in the last weeks of school. The school system follows a strict lecture-test-repeat model leading up to a larger exam at the end of the semester.

My Indian athletes were experts at exams and were taught at a young age how to recite information with distinct precision under high stress. I recognized the similarities in the command-obey dynamic for my young players on the pitch and the command-obey dynamic found in the classroom. This was important to observe because it meant that a command-obey mindset would probably be reinforced with existing and incoming players.

In India, the value of education is unlike most other countries. Anything which would distract from academic excellence was met with a bit of reluctance. We had a team of high school players who advanced to a prestigious tournament in Singapore but declined because it happened to fall on the same week of school exams. Imagine this scenario played out in other parts of the world? The dedication and work ethic of the Indian student is remarkable and highly admirable. With academics at the forefront of all social status and career options, until very recently, athletics in India were widely considered only a pastime and a hobby.

I began to think of different ways that I could parlay the educational values in Indian culture into our success in the sports industry. I kept my thoughts and ideas about collaborative ownership from Sweden in the back of my mind as I spent time building relationships with my teams, learning the culture, and asking a bazillion questions to clarify vision and values within the team. After time in intentional observation, I was ready to begin leading small changes in our academy by getting more specific and strategic in our action steps towards our goals.

Nearby Science Park to encourage STEM learning

Part II
Ownership Culture

Chapter Four
Ownership Culture

In our team, I specifically identified the command-obey nature of our training to be the biggest impact on challenges in performance. I could be wrong, but it was my best assessment at the time. From my observations, I believed a better culture of ownership in our training could change the dynamic of our academies for the better.

In application, this transformation towards collaborative ownership on the pitch looked like this:

Rather than "Stand in a line, kick a ball, wait for direction," I would provide challenges like, "In a game scenario, when you pass, kick, or shoot; you will have to know how to kick with power and precision for better ball control and possession. So from here, I want you to kick the ball to knock down those three cones. To do this successfully, you will have to kick with power and precision."

This does not seem like a big transition. Certainly not transformational in communication. On a surface level, it's hardly any difference at all. In both scenarios, the players are challenged to kick the ball. However, there *is* a massive difference.

The transformation is in the focus. In the first challenge, the focus is on the coach. Players know they are successful because the coach tells them they are successful. They are focused on kicking the ball exactly the way the coach taught them rather than actually meeting the goal. It is from this focus many players will turn to the sideline during a match before the play is complete.

In the second challenge, the focus is on the cones (goal). The focus on the goal allows the player to know if he/she has been successful in their challenge. The coach is merely a guide.

The source of innovation, progression, and ownership stems from the focus point. The individual voices in achieving a goal are more apt to be drowned out if leaders are the only focus.

In the first challenge, players know how to kick the ball in a specific way but may not know how to adjust and apply in match scenarios. What are the progressions? How can we adjust? How can we improve? If the focus is on the coach, the *coach* will likely provide improvement, progression, and innovative solutions.

In the second challenge, players know many ways to kick the ball (effective and ineffective) and understand how each method applies in the game. The *player* is focused on the goal and can improve, experiment, try progressions and advance with innovative solutions. Players tried kicking with their left foot, right foot, in-foot, laces, running up to the ball and standing still, they tried to knock down all of the cones in one sweep and tried knocking down cones one at a time. I would alter the challenge by spreading the cones farther apart, adding more cones, creating a greater distance between player and cones, and making competitions to see who could kick down the cones first.

One player excitedly told me he practiced this activity at his home with soda pop bottles to improve his precision in kicking for better passes during matches. Another practiced from longer distances in the vacant lot near his home to improve his ability to kick with power for stronger accurate distance kicks during matches. This slight alteration in verbiage gave a big shift in focus and application. The players were coming up with progressions on their own and seeing the application.

In many work teams, a misguided focus might manifest itself in unwavering policy practices, strict manuals, and "my-way-or-the-highway" approaches. A simple way to identify misguided focus is to observe team members during unconventional situations. Does the team remain unwavering in a prison of policy and single approach manual, or do they have the flexibility to adapt, adjust, and be creative in their problem solving to best achieve the desired end result?

What is the difference? It's not just culture. It's specifically a culture of ownership. It's a company with a clearly defined *why* and *what* with opportunity for ownership within the *how*. It's a company which provides opportunities for ownership and "allows people the freedom to be human." (Moon et al.) One team may focus on the task, another may focus on the goal.

Clarifying *what* and *why* is important but it does not in itself establish competitive advantage. *How* your *what* and *why* are pursued differentiates a winning team from a mediocre one.

Organizationally, my thoughts moved beyond football as I thought of a dozen different hospitals that have a vision of excellent patient care; I thought of a plethora of financial institutions that have a core value of stewardship; and nearly every educational institution that has a goal of student success. These are not bad directions and should be driving industry focus... but industry values and standards are not the driving forces that make teams uniquely better—they are the minimum standard to stay in the game, not win championships.

Furthermore, I thought of how all people have a goal of financial freedom, many have a vision of healthy relationships, and a slew of folks have a mission of good physical health. These are fantastic values and goals, but I wondered if most people long for financial stability, healthy relationships, and good health, and if most industries long for quality service, stewardship, and growth...why aren't all succeeding if all have the right agreed-upon *what* and *why*?

Purpose and defined outcomes are critical and lay a foundation for success, but competitive advantage is not found in this alone. I coached several teams throughout the years with a similar vision of player success in goals on and off the pitch but not all were equally successful. What made some teams better than the rest? What was their advantage?

Competitive advantage lies not within the vision cast- but within the ownership of action towards the vision. Most desire healthy relationships, excellent customer service, and proper stewardship, but the difference between desiring and achieving success is in the ownership of action. Everybody gets somewhere; few people get there on purpose. The ownership of action defines the success towards the vision.

As a leader, it was my job to consistently and adamantly clarify the *why* and the *what*.

My role as a leader is to clarify our focus. Then, my job was to equip my players with the resources and skills to take ownership in the *how*. I should not be the main focus - the purpose should be front and center.

Too often, leaders communicate the *what* and the *how*, leading to a forgotten *why*, a hushed team with diluted ownership, and unclear purpose. By communicating the *why* and the *what*, the purpose of action is reinstated and the team is given a true opportunity to establish competitive advantage through the *how*.

We altered our training to refocus from the coach to the goal. We refocused from perfecting a challenge to applying the challenge lessons to the match. We redirected ownership from exclusively the coach to the player.

When the coach is in control and the players don't have elasticity to move, the game looks more like foosball. In foosball, the ball can get stagnant if action is not within reach for players because they are unable to move from the pole. There is very little agility for players to move outside of a specific lane. Players have limited ability, mobility, and control. With ownership of action, teams could transform from foosball to football.

What does ownership actually look like?

In India, strict lines, laps, and lectures were the driving force of our academies. Sometimes, we owned the process, other times it appeared the process owned us.

The process dictated *what* we did and *how* we did it. Players would be quick to run to a position and promptly outline the "lane" of each position. This was great when learning overall zone coverage but led to awkward abrupt stops when the ball went outside of the player's "lane" in the course of a play. I had a player who loved to play left wing but would not move even a few steps towards the center of the pitch to get the ball in fear he might be out of position. He played on the outside "lane" and knew his place. He would not budge during a match even if the ball was nearest to him but outside his lane which led to loss of possession. The process of being in field position wasn't necessarily bad, but the strict role and policy was detrimental to adjustments, exceptions, and creativity.

The term "people over processes" has become a common saying among certain circles involving organizational culture. For most organizations, it simply means an allowed level of latitude for the humanity in an organization to shine.

A risk with the mantra "people over processes" is it can put us in a position to disregard processes altogether. In reality, processes are really important! I believe that a better mantra should be "people own processes." The process is very important but it is not more important than the end-goal.

Ownership began with messaging and communication. I tried to be intentional to bring clarity to ownership opportunities.

When I first came to the academies, the conversation was about the *what* and the *how*. Kick the ball; kick it like this.

Now, the conversation turned to *why* and *what*. We must pass, kick, and shoot with power and precision during a match to maintain possession for opportunities to score and defend goals. Let's practice by kicking with power and precision during this challenge.

This was not a complete overhaul in communication—it was a slight pivot.

Coaching is about equipping players with the tools they need to accomplish their goals.

Every day, I had the opportunity to add or take away tools through my communication and training. If I direct one single way to kick the ball, I am eliminating so many other possible methods of kicking. Every day I would ask myself, "Are you increasing or limiting the resources in your team's toolbox?"

Naturally, there are aspects of any industry and any organization which restrict complete opportunities for ownership. I would not want complete autonomy with loose rules or regulations in most industries including transportation, healthcare, and food. As I coached football, there were aspects of the game and aspects of our training curriculum that could not be altered. I couldn't change the number of players allowed on the pitch during a match, pitch size in a match, the amount of balls or goalie positions on the pitch. However, I found there were at least four different opportunities in which I could provide ownership for my players. These opportunities span beyond the football pitch into nearly every industry, organization, and team.

The four main opportunities for ownership are in processes, methods, projects, and roles. We weren't only owning our processes. I furthered the mantra with other opportunities for ownership to include "people own methods," "people own projects," and "people own roles."

Opportunities for ownership

- Processes
- Methods
- Projects
- Roles

I began implementing small pivots to strategically empower small wins for more ownership in our team. Each team was different and embraced ownership opportunities through a slight adjustment in communication and focus with various levels of acceptance. As our teams continued to progress in training, we explored how we could be uniquely better in each opportunity for ownership.

Chapter Five
Opportunities for Ownership in Processes

After my age-twelve players had learned the different positions and responsibilities on the pitch, I gave them the opportunity to make their own formations and assigned positions for end-of-session scrimmages. This exercise allowed the players to experiment with different formations (a 4-4-2 formation versus a 4-3-3 formation and so on), try different positions, and increase overall understanding of the game. I would give the players a few minutes to come up with their positions and formations as a team and then we would begin to play.

During one session, I gave this challenge to one of my teams and at the end of three minutes I saw a goalie in the box and ten strikers. All of the players wanted to score goals in this single position. Nobody wanted to play any other position. I smiled and asked the team about the opportunities they could create with their use of space. "MissAmberMam, we all want to score goals. Plus, he's a good goalie." Fair enough.

I let them play for a few minutes in deep frustration as they ran into each other and were ill-positioned against the opposing team. We continued to scrimmage a little longer and then I paused play to allow the team to make any adjustments. The players looked around the pitch in bewilderment. They wanted to be strikers, but they could not all play the same position and play most effectively. They needed different roles.

One player went to defender, another went to midfield, and slowly the players went to various parts of the pitch. When the movement seemed to stop, I asked the same question about different opportunities created using space and the players had many answers. Players now saw the value of each position and the importance of staying in a somewhat agreed-upon formation. While there were times I assigned positions, exercises such as these were a different process by which we made a decision. Through this decision-making process, we increased game understanding and saw the power of each person on the team. We established competitive advantage by clarifying the processes within our team.

Similar process - clarity practices revolve around organizations every day. I remembered reading how Whole Foods Supermarket transformed their Human Resources hiring process to allow a uniquely better culture of ownership. *Hawaii Business Magazine* writes, "Whole Foods started a program in which new hires were voted in or out by their teams after their first 90 days (for part timers) or 45 days (for full timers) at the company. Seventy-five percent of the team needs to participate in the vote, and a two-thirds majority of those voting is required to keep an employee on board. But new hires aren't just thrown in front of their peers for review. From the start, new employees work with a team educator who helps them navigate the job. New employees get weekly feedback from managers and detailed checklists that clearly outline what's expected of the employee. So when they're up for a vote, they're in a great position to be accepted by their teams." (Fox et. al.)

Think about the amount of ownership each member of the team has in their Human Resources process. This is not a process which owns the team, but rather a team who owns the process. They are given ownership by being given a voice. Lack of clarity in processes can lead to ambiguity in ownership. Establish competitive advantage through process clarity in your organization.

Keep in mind, process ownership goes beyond decision making. You can also provide opportunities for ownership in the process of task completion.

On the pitch, I looked at our process of practicing passing. We stood and kicked back and forth with accuracy and precision. This challenge was efficient, but without progressions it was not like a match scenario. I instructed our players to get into micro teams of 2-4 players then challenged them to keep possession of the ball. Attaining and maintaining possession is critical in football - it would be difficult to score goals if we didn't have the ball. We would practice this through challenging games with clearly defined outcomes like "try to complete 10 passes without losing possession." From challenge progressions like these, players were able to experiment *how* to complete the task while understanding the game application.

Here, we went beyond completing a single task (passing the ball) to concentrating on overall goal success (attain and maintain possession). The players had ownership opportunities in how they would pass, progress, and keep possession. While the simple process of passing a ball might seem menial, when applied on a large scale, process ownership of completing a task can be revolutionary. One way that you can increase process ownership of task completion is by streamlining your processes. Eliminating excess and waste will allow opportunities for your team to concentrate on what really matters.

American food chain powerhouse McDonalds did not build its legacy in position nor in product, but in revolutionizing the process of preparing and serving food. The original McDonald's brothers were uniquely better by devising a system which allowed them to serve food in 30 seconds. People flocked to their store for speedy service and a good hamburger. By improving the process of preparing hamburgers through meticulous ownership of process improvement, the McDonalds brothers revolutionized fast food. (Hancock) The McDonalds brothers did this by streamlining the process so that team members could act with proficiency and confidence in their role.

In addition to clarifying process ownership of decision making and streamlining process ownership of task completion, our players also took ownership in the process of their movement and agility.

To a non-footballer, ball movement in football seems straightforward - go towards the goal. However, every team has a unique approach in how they move the ball to create opportunities to score goals. There is an immense opportunity for ownership in the process of achieving this goal.

We tried new approaches and processes of moving the ball to create opportunities on the pitch. We did not try to be like any other team; we were trying to find the best form of ball movement that highlighted the strengths and skills of our team. We sought to own a process that would make us uniquely better.

Sometimes, the conversations in discovering our best process were interesting. Every Tuesday and Thursday on the football pitch, I went as the American coach working alongside an Englishman coach for a French Football Academy at a Canadian International School in India. The cross-cultural situations provided some interesting, awkward, and sometimes outright hilarious moments.

During one session, we were teaching the players about transitioning from one end of the pitch to the other without passing through the middle part of the pitch (crossing the field) and several of the players quickly replied, "Ah, yes. Sublimation."

".........excuse me?"

"You know, Coach. Sublimation. The phase transition of a substance directly from the solid to the gas phase without passing through the intermediate liquid phase. We are going from one phase to another without the intermediary."

"Ah, yes. Today we are going to practice sublimation on the field."

It was then that the English coach and I realized we were all speaking English yet we were speaking completely different languages. We understood concepts differently, which provided opportunities to share ideas and create unique processes altogether. It was really important to be straightforward in our training.

Rather than dive into deep complicated plays, we sought to simplify ideas of ball movement to be more approachable and digestible so players could put the concepts into action with confidence. We put the fundamentals first and sought to be excellent in our foundation above all else. Complicated training can distract from what is important - focus on the fundamentals. You can increase ownership of processes within your team by simplifying processes.

Similar to ball movement, corporate teams can increase ownership of movement by simplifying complex, confusing, overwhelming processes. Complexity jades clarity and the more complicated a process becomes, the more opportunity for ambiguity and inefficiencies in processes. Southwest Airlines simplified their processes through different methods such as eliminating seat selection, utilizing a single model airplane, and simplified booking on the website. Employees feel more empowered to take ownership of something that is easily understood.

Through owned processes, our players were able to increase engagement, understanding, and performance. They became more confident in their decisions and clearer in their understanding. We increased people's ownership of processes by simplifying, streamlining and increasing understanding of the processes within our team.

Process ownership in decision making, task completion, and movements towards our goals all began with a simple shift in communication from *what* and *how,* to *what* and *why* - with opportunities for ownership in the *how* of our processes. From sublimation to field positions, to a delicious hamburger; process ownership can make up the personality and uniquely better aspect of the team. You can create opportunities for process ownership within your team through streamlined processes, simplified processes, and processes that are easy to understand. Oftentimes, murky complicated processes are the root of un-owned processes. As I was teaching process ownership on the pitch, I was also learning the different and unique processes India owned in real life.

Process Ownership in India

One evening, my friend Sanjana told me we would not be having work the next day because there was a bandh. I asked her what a bandh was and she replied, "It means everything will shut down." She told me bandh in Hindi literally means "shut down."

I thought, "Okay, cool. It's like a holiday. I'll go to the park, maybe walk around, and do a little sightseeing." I woke up the next morning to an apocalyptic silence. It was the first time that I would experience the eerie silence that the world would encounter in later years during the 2020 COVID-19 shutdowns. That's when I realized I had a very incorrect idea of a bandh. I was told to stay inside. It could be dangerous for me to go out.

From the land of Gandhi, bandh is a type of civil protest. The city will shut down for a day or two in solidarity for the community or political party to speak. During a bandh, the general public stays inside, commerce and public transportation cease, and the entire city goes on lockdown. This is a powerful tool because of its impact on the local economy. It's an owned process of diplomatic protest unique to India.

Though largely peaceful, burglary, arson attacks, stoning, and clashes between the bandh organizers and the police are common enough during a bandh. I figured as long as I stayed inside and was literally outside of a stone's throw from the action, I would be safe. Nevertheless, images of 27 burning buses, broken windows, and massive protests were a little unsettling in this country rightfully known for peace.

This particular bandh was over the dispute of water allocation for farming areas versus city dwelling areas. I sought to educate myself as much as possible on the topic and tried to be an informed guest in the country. Some countries protest with marches, petitions, and lobbyists. India utilizes traditional forms of protest in addition to a uniquely owned process of communicating disagreement.

My biggest challenge during the bandh was access to food.

With markets and restaurants closed, we had little food in the house. I had six eggs, two bananas, and an apple. This is all I ate for three days.

We had hired a new coach from England named Chris who was passionate about football and we instantly became friends. We shared many ideas about coaching in youth development. Chris had previous international academy coaching experience and I was excited to learn from him. He became a great mentor and friend in coaching youth football. He had been in India a few weeks when we experienced our first bandh.

The day that the bandh was lifted Chris, Sanjana, and I dressed up and went to a restaurant for a hearty feast.

The next day I went to the store and bought a few nonperishable food items to keep in my room in case of another bandh. We had several that year.

India took ownership of the process of protesting and reframed it to include a complete economic shutdown. This was a way that India took ownership to be uniquely effective in communicating the magnitude of importance the public felt towards a cause, and it sought to speed up the political process of action. India illustrated the lessons of process ownership that I was learning on the pitch - they had a streamlined, clarified, and adapted to new forms of protest.

With the ownership lessons from the bandh in mind, I sought to take ownership of my personal process of communication as I tried to best lead my team. I asked myself, "Could I communicate in a unique way to better reach my audience?" I looked specifically into ways that I could simplify, clarify, or adapt my coaching to better serve my team.

I began a process of asking my players questions about their goals on and off the field. Asking questions about my player's non-football aspirations was a great way to build relationships and a fantastic opportunity to reiterate the vision of success on and off the pitch. For parents who were learning how to support the balance of academics and athletics, hearing our conversations about how the two can complement each other was a powerful dialogue and streamlined the connection from sports to life.

I had a 10-year old player named Tejas who wanted to be an astronaut. He was taking classes and learning about astrophysics to meet his goal. We built connections from his professional and athletic goals. Astronauts must pass astronaut training. We connected the physical challenges, the communication, the problem solving, and the teamwork in football to his future goals of completing his astronaut training.

I had a young girl named Shreya who wanted to be a neurosurgeon. We talked about the importance of hard work, dedication, commitment, focus, drive, perseverance, leadership, and teamwork required for her to be a great neurosurgeon and how she had the opportunity to practice all of these principles on the football pitch.

Providing extra layers of purpose and meaning to both football goals and long-term career goals created a momentum in our training. We openly discussed how we could use our strengths, skills, passions, and abilities to be an excellent team. As a coach, I increased my communication to be more effective in our training through streamlining "goals conversations", clarifying focus on strengths, and adapting to new cultural references.

As I learned Hindi, I would include little phrases into my training such as, "ek, do, teen, chalo!" (1, 2, 3, go!) I would yell as we raced around the field, "Jaldi! Hurry, hurry, chicken curry!" for my non-veg (non-vegetarian) players or "Hurry, hurry, pani puri!" for my veg players. As we scored, we celebrated with our best Bollywood dance moves I had learned from Bolly-aerobics and my Bollywood movie marathons.

In your organization, you can establish competitive advantage by simplifying processes through lean practices, clarifying processes through comprehendable approaches, and increasing adaptability of processes.

Masala dosa and chai

Chapter Six
Method Ownership

I began a session by explaining, "In a game we must be agile, quick, and have strong ball control so let's have a race and see who can dribble around 5 cones the fastest." This was a slight adjustment from, "Go around the cones like this."

I would progress the challenges further by adding obstacles to encourage problem solving rather than directed solutions. I would add obstacles to the cone-dribbling game such as you can't use your inside right foot, you can't use the laces, and so forth. Through these challenges, players found the solution that worked best for them and shared their new ideas with other team members.

I did not give a directive on how to specifically kick the ball. Rather, I communicated the goal (go quickly around the cones) and the why (to be quick and agile with ball control in game situations). The *what* and *why* created a firm framework for flexibility within the *how*.

You can increase ownership of methods (and processes for that matter) by increasing the opportunity for agility. Stagnant methods of task completion can lead to irrelevant, uncompetitive, and outdated practices. The agility in our methods of training allowed us to adapt and adjust our performance during matches.

Teams can become more agile by implementing faster iterations of change through smaller adjustments.

In our academies, a good coach would not present a challenge activity without first identifying the *why* and *what*. Then, she/he would create smaller iterations of progressions within the training challenges. We would ask the question in our instructional design, "How do we progress from completing this challenge?" For the ball-around-the-cones game, players had more opportunities to practice problem-solving, innovation, and skill development as I progressed the challenge level by increasing the amount of cones, adjusting time limits, creating obstacles, or limiting options. Most importantly, players knew how these challenges could apply in match scenarios. We did not dramatically jump from one activity to the next. We built upon the momentum of one activity and we understood how the skills could apply to another activity for match preparation.

We would create a series of challenges and skill practices and break them down into smaller activities. The shorter iterations of change would increase the momentum of training and adaptability. In time, players would insert their own progressions as we continued to build a growth mindset. Identifying progressions and application became a habit as we increased training agility through shorter iterations of change with faster feedback loops.

Similar to our training methods, you can increase the agility within your organization to create a better method of development. For example, at British Telecom the team decided to adapt agile methods by implementing shorter user stories for more manageable and quality timelines, directly involving customers to quicken approvals, and implementing shorter iterations for faster feedback loops.

How did this impact the team? Within two years the delivery cycle improved from 12 months to 90 days. The quality increased as measured with success markers at the end of every cycle and the developer morale improved. (Krush, 2018)

Notice the *why* and the *what* did not necessarily change with the new method. However, the altered *how* transformed the competitiveness of the company.

You can increase ownership of methods by adapting a more agile framework through shorter iterations of change. While many of the approaches to ownership have been focused on efficiency design, we should also deeply consider how to increase ownership through personalized practices.

For example, *how* a message is communicated is just as important as what is communicated. A team that communicates in person is going to have a different dynamic than those whose relationships are behind a screen. A straightforward, direct communication style or method is different from a more casual or indirect approach.

Our program managers in Bangalore believed the most effective form of communication was to call every single player individually. Furthermore, none had voicemail. We had to continue to call until we received an in-real-time answer.

While an inconvenience, the new communication method dramatically affected our team dynamic for the better. This method of communication challenged me to build deeper relationships with my parents and players because it was an intentional time to have individual conversations. Sure, I spoke to people before and after sessions, at team building events, and at tournaments, but this was an opportunity to speak more candidly. Our method of communication helped define our academy's culture.

This led to really powerful conversations and gave me insight into how I should alter my coaching methods according to the team dynamic. Keep in mind, I was coaching various players and teams across the city six days a week and my learning curve altered with each location, team, and caliber of play. Each location I coached was a little different.

With Gameday Academy, I coached at a new turf pitch about two hours away with traffic. Most of the players at this location were from the community and would walk, take a car, rickshaw, or bike to come to sessions. The players were interested in football and had beginner to upper mid-level skill. We created a ladder in which a player could earn the opportunity to move up to more skilled and experienced teams. Parents were very excited to watch their kids pursue their interest and generally saw this opportunity as a fun extracurricular activity.

We had a large program that I occasionally coached for with Paris Saint Germain which was a more focussed team. The players here meant business and were dedicated to their craft. The parents were extremely invested and the expectations for performance were high.

I also coached for many Paris Saint Germain teams and Gameday Academy teams at several international schools. The facilities were the caliber of a large university except it was intended for elementary through high school students.

Many of the players at international schools were from various backgrounds. Between parental influence, heritage diversity, and geographic residence, players at the international schools had a tremendous wealth of knowledge, references, and uncanny wit that was unusual for their age. I found myself using vocabulary from three to seven different languages and referencing cultures, holidays, and celebrations from all over the world on a regular basis.

Each coaching location was dramatically different and I had to adjust my style, expectations, and approach to talent development with each new team.

As I spoke on the phone to the player's and parents, I was able to give clear updates on progress and goals and reiterate our academy vision. One conversation that I had with a player's father from an international school exemplified such class that I wrote the short monologue in my journal. It was widely known that his son was the best in skill on the pitch and a true leader on the team.

I gave a call to check in and give an update and the father's response impressed me. "MissAmberMam, my son aspires to be a professional footballer, to play in Europe in the Premier League. I believe if he is determined and trains properly, he can do this and I support him in his dream. But that is not my focus. I care more about his development as a person than as a player. I have done everything I know to exemplify character, determination, prudence, trustworthiness, and respect in my life for him and have obviously brought him to this prestigious school to learn as well. I want you to know his aspirations, but I also want you to know our values and want to make sure that they are put first and not compromised. A professional athlete without character and life skills would be a failure on my part."

We had spoken previously about our vision and values, but I was shaken by this father's conviction and told him we would do our best in partnership to invest into the life of his son. Conversations of encouragement, reiterated goals, concerns, tension, life events, and relationships often happened with this altered method of communication from a mass email to a personal phone call. While not as efficient, it was incredibly effective.

Streamlining processes and methods can increase efficiency and clarity in the organization. Sometimes, over-automation or robust-simplification has the potential to eliminate a meaningful aspect of the organizational culture - the human aspect. This experience inspired me to ask more meaningful questions as I was leading our training. I wanted to make sure that in my quest to be more efficient in our sessions, I was not eliminating quality. I would ask myself of our process and method refinements, "Does this eliminate distractions?" "Does this eliminate focus?" "How does this add value?" "Does this take away value?" Was it worthwhile to save a few hours every month by sending an email if it eliminated intentional time to check in and have a meaningful conversation with each player/parent?

Methods of communication can affect any organization. I recalled a time in the United States when I joined a new company and was working on a few projects in which I communicated ideas and questions with the team members through email as I had done in previous teams. In the first week, I became a little frustrated because all my emails were going unanswered.

I asked a team member about the emails. He chuckled and said the primary form of communication in their team was not email. In fact, email was hardly used as a form of communication at all. This team communicated through the Slack app. I began to send my questions and ideas through the app and received almost instant replies.

With this slight shift in communication method from email to Slack, the formal manner in which I was sending the messages soon turned to a more relaxed and casual tone. Team members would respond with "Like" functions, memes, and gifs in addition to written replies. The method of communication within our team created the culture and set the tone for our team dynamics. Whether it's in-person meetings, phone calls, texts, emails, or Instant Messaging, the method of communication can affect the culture of the team. In your team, make methods personal.

As I continued challenging ownership methods, I discovered that method ownership went beyond task completion and communication into achieving and exceeding goals. We had increased ownership of methods within our team to be uniquely better by adapting a more agile framework and implementing more personal practices. We also increased ownership by encouraging diverse approaches to methods within the team.

Sometimes, I would teach various methods of ball handling techniques (in-foot, out-foot, laces, sole) to younger players then challenge the players to see who could get 100 touches on the ball first.

I watched as some would start with the sole of their foot, then move to laces and then move to in-foot and so forth as they tried different ways to get 100 touches on the ball first. The method was linked to the goal of efficiency and quickness on the ball to be swift against opponents. Players refined their skill, discovered their strengths, and found the most efficient way to complete the challenge while understanding their application of the tools.

Method ownership went beyond touches on the football. I coached players who took ownership of their methods to throw-in the ball. This was their opportunity to be uniquely better and add competitive value to the team. I once coached a player who could throw the ball nearly 35 yards down the pitch with ease and control.

The player's secret did not lie within his strength (which was immense) but rather in his throwing method he had learned from three older brothers in cricket. He concocted his own method of throwing that highlighted the power of cricket but stayed within the legality of football rules. It took him a few tries to learn a legal throw, but once he learned - he was nearly unstoppable. This type of method ownership was a specific way to be uniquely better.

You can increase ownership of methods in your team by building upon players' different strengths and skills. Define the skills of your team, the methods and approaches that are currently being used, and expand them. Upskilling your talent through a variety of training, feedback, and opportunities for new applications can increase confidence and ownership of development. Organizational ownership grows at the speed of talent capability. In your team, identify the skills of your talent and intentionally build upon them.

Ownership opportunities in our methods created a space for us to be uniquely better in our performance and establish a competitive advantage for success. You can create opportunities for ownership within your methods by adapting a more agile framework for quicker iterations of change, deeply considering the human impact of methods in your team, and encouraging/ expanding a variety of methods in your organization.

India's Method Ownership

Outside of the pitch, extreme method ownership was exemplified on a grand scale when India took ownership in methods of combating corruption. In this challenge, many businesses also took full ownership of payment methods after India's Prime Minister Modi stated India would be demonetized.

In simple terms, India is a mostly cash nation and many were falsifying tax documents to claim they had made less money in order to keep the excess money illegally without taxation. One evening, Prime Minister Modi declared all Indian currency larger than 100 rupee (equivalent to about $1.25 in 2016) would no longer be considered a valid form of currency. This was effective immediately.

We would have to exchange our money by either depositing the entirety of our cash into the bank and using an ATM to withdraw necessary funds a little at a time, *or* we could exchange roughly the equivalent of 30 USD at a time at the bank. Either way, if someone tried to deposit or exchange more than what was declared on their taxes the individual would be caught for tax fraud and fined at 200%. Everyone had until December 31st to exchange their money. After that, the old Indian rupees would be worth no more than monopoly bills.

I woke up that morning to discover the results of the United States presidential election and I mistakenly thought that would be the big news story for the day. Then, I looked out the window to find hours-long lines at the bank, I found people burning bags of money in the streets and openly feeding it to the animals (it was worse for people to have the money and pay the tax than burn it openly), I found my normal food vendors and street markets in a hustle (everyone was rationing their valid rupees). I realized all of my money was in large bills and I had no money to buy food for breakfast. It was chaos. I wondered how I would eat and function in the coming days.

As an international resident, this was an additional problem-solving opportunity. I did not want to open a bank account in India, and many of the bankers were hesitant about exchanging money for foreigners. In the first week, I sat in a line at a non-air-conditioned, sweaty bank in an upper room for six hours only to have the banker tell me he would not exchange my bills because I wasn't an Indian citizen. I don't know if there was a reason; I think bankers were just trying to do their best.

In a way, this was Prime Minister Modi's method of ownership in detecting tax fraud and addressing corruption. It was one of the boldest political moves I've ever witnessed by a government leader. Most people, though inconvenienced, were initially mainly supportive of demonetization because they appreciated a bold move to address corruption. The method was certainly unconventional and unique.

In the aftermath of demonetization, I began to see posters and advertisements about debit cards, credits cards, and a PayPal equivalent called Paytm. These advertisements were education-focused, informing the populous about different methods of payment. I saw one advertisement that literally explained how a debit card worked. It's not that Indian people didn't know about cards and online payments, it just wasn't widely used.

Remember, India is also a dramatically diverse place with people from all walks of life. Especially for the underserved populations, I saw advertisements that read, "Help your help," alluding to helping the service workers in the home in navigating this new financial landscape.

Many people had creative and impressive solutions to these demonetization challenges, the most impressive adjustments I saw was with local vendors. I saw the fruit man with his cart of bananas, pineapples, and watermelon selling his goods via card, Paytm, *or* cash. Businesses that were cash only found themselves adjusting to multiple payment methods and increasing business through their multiple methods of service. The process of payment was essentially the same, but the method was different. Those businesses that were agile and quick to adjust their payment methods significantly benefited from the shake-up.

Rather than payment methods owning and dictating businesses, businesses took back ownership by altering and adjusting payment methods to create more ownership and competitive advantage.

I thought of the lessons I could learn from demonitization that I could apply on the pitch. I began to include more opportunities for agility and quick problem solving within our sessions.

I would add and take away resources (an extra defender, zone restrictions, goal position) to challenge the players to adjust and be creative in adverse situations. This method of problem solving training built up our agility and quick wit on the pitch during matches.

Whether it's methods in communication, task completion, or decision making; there are different methods to improve performance as a team. I continued to work with players on the pitch to find their best methods of play in which they could take full ownership and thrive.

The market in India

What is the difference between the methods and processes?

While the four different opportunities for ownership may run together at times, processes and methods are oftentimes used interchangeably and many have asked me the difference between the two.

A method is the *how* of completing a goal while a process is the *series of hows* to complete a goal. While the method may dramatically impact the process and vice versa, the two are not always interchangeable.

We kicked the ball with a specific in-foot, out-foot, or laces method. The method is generally a one level challenge or task. The process of how we moved the ball around the pitch required a series of kicks. The process could have variation depending on the method, but not necessarily. The two are complimentary but not the same.

Similarly, hiring interview methods may consist of panel interviews, one-on-one interviews, a test, or a skills review. These are examples of different methods to review applicants. This is different from the hiring interview process which could consist of a series of interviews. The hiring process could take a couple of weeks and could be multi-layered. Your hiring method is more specific to how you approach the steps in the hiring process.

Relatedly, you may have an effective interview method that is a part of an ineffective interview process. Let's say that you conduct insightful, meaningful interviews but operate under an interview process that is inefficient with long lag times in communication. You may have an interview process which contains ineffective interview methods. This means that you could have an extremely efficient interview process with poor interview methods that do not allow the interviewer to gain needed information to make an informed decision.

Another example would be my family's chocolate chip cookie recipe. My grandmother, mom, and myself have the exact same recipe in the family cookbook. We have the same instructions and process that we follow. However, our cookies do not all taste the same. Why? Our methods in following the process are different. When I mix the batter, I whisk the batter in a back and forth motion, my mom whisks the batter in a small circular motion, and my grandmother whisks the batter in a large circular motion. We all are following the same process of mixing batter in our instructions to bake cookies - but our methods are a little different.

The two greatly affect one another but they are not, in fact, the same. Methods and processes both offer opportunities for ownership to establish competitive advantage. As I continued to coach the teams in India, I discovered that the opportunities for ownership did not end with processes and methods. There were more opportunities to increase ownership in our team.

Chapter Seven
Project Ownership

Within our training sessions, we would include opportunities for ownership on a micro level, building up to larger ownership opportunities.

Our sessions followed a pretty basic routine.

- Warm-up activity to get physically and mentally ready
- Activity 1 to introduce or develop a skill or concept starting with a foundation and increasing progressions
- Activity 2 to progress and apply the skill or concept in match examples
- Scrimmage with a focus on the day's lesson
- Gather for a debrief of the lesson, discuss take-aways, and give two sprints down and back (this was the final opportunity to "leave it all out on the pitch" and was a signal that the session was over)

Within this framework, I would sometimes begin a session by explaining to my players, "We need to warm up to prepare our mind and our muscles to play football; how should we do that?" The players would choose one of the warm-up games that we had already learned in previous sessions or they made up their own games that achieved the goal of warming up the muscles and mind in a simple 5 to 10 minute project-ownership activity.

Projects can include any event, initiative, or project with a beginning and an end. Processes and methods are ongoing, projects have an intentional time to stop and reflect. This is critical in recognizing wins.

You can implement projects on a micro and a mega level in your organization to increase ownership. Within our training sessions, we would have mini projects of picking up gear, organizing our team for scrimmages, and competing in challenges. We saw tournaments and matches as larger projects.

I went to a tournament with one team filled with excitement and some nervousness. I reiterated the team training and preparation that had led to this tournament day. This was their moment. It was up to them to have confidence in their tools, skills, and abilities to win the match.

The project of a massive tournament could overwhelm the team. You can increase project ownership by breaking down large projects into smaller micro projects to build momentum, small wins, and quicker improvement. We broke down the project of a tournament into match halves. We would focus all of our energy on doing our best for one half of a match. This created short focus sprints and faster feedback loops so that we could be more agile in our match improvements. We would celebrate, debrief, and learn from one half before starting the next half. If we had four matches in a tournament, we did this for eight halves.

This was an important mindset framework, especially for the second halves of matches. If we were winning at half time, I did not want our players to get overconfident and blow a lead. Score was zero-zero. We had to play well for two full halves. If we were losing at half time, I didn't want players to be discouraged and give up. We had an entire other half to play. Score was zero-zero.

This mindset shift resulted in faster improvement, better focus, and more match victories.

Emphasizing player ownership re-focused project success from the coach to the players. Success came from the entirety of the team. Players began to look inwards and toward other team members for team success. I was not the only person with answers. When people own the answers, they are often more confident and dedicated to the solutions.

Success would be less likely if I would have entered the teams into challenging tournaments without their input or buy in. Instead, I tried to create an environment to build their confidence in their skills, abilities, and talent. The team grew enthusiastic about the challenge of more matches and proposed tournaments on their own accord. The types of projects that you take on in your team influences the culture and standards within your team. A team that does not embrace challenges or prefers exclusively small projects will have a different culture than a team that takes on bold, innovative, and difficult challenges.

Our team was intentional to take on projects that reiterated our academy values. You can increase ownership within your team by taking on projects that align with your overall *why*.

Project Ownership in India

My job and purpose consisted of helping India become a great football nation. I took on several projects outside of my immediate job description to help fulfill that purpose and increase our competitive edge as a team. While the kids were learning how to take ownership of their projects on the pitch, I was working on a series of projects related to sports outside of the academies.

I was asked to come to the Indian National Sports Conference in Hyderabad, Telangana. There were a couple hundred people

at the event and I met a community of wonderful professionals that were passionate about transforming India into a great
sports nation.

I walked in the conference room and felt the eyes of wonder
and inquisition follow my moves as I tried to inconspicuously
sit in the corner. After announcements, the host invited me to
stand up and share from where I had come. I replied, "My name
is Amber, and I live in Karnataka." At this response, many eyes
lit up. The man with the microphone pressed again. Where was
I *really* from? I replied, "Karnataka is home where I live, but I
was raised in the United States." I had a million welcomes and
hellos. I spent the next four days meeting with people and sharing ideas and inspiration about sport.

After one of our conference sessions, I walked into the mess
hall, filled my plate with the spicy, delicious food, and began
eating with my right hand. Suddenly, the room seemed to stop
and I felt more than a dozen camera phones take pictures of
this blonde-headed American acting outside of her stereotype.
The days were filled with lines for photos with me and people
wanting my contact information which expanded my network of
resources. This fanfare was becoming the norm. In fact, another
time in Chennai, a man interrupted the photo line and demanded
a fee before anyone else could take pictures with me. People
paid and I felt unsure about a random person benefiting from my
blondness. It's the closest to celebrity status that I'll ever feel.

On the last day of the conference, all the sports professionals from my home state of Karnataka gave me a state T-shirt. We
all took a photo with our matching shirts as the sports ambas-
sadors for Karnataka. Projects like these were so worthwhile.

It was at events like these that I met a girl named Shauna,
a football coach for underserved communities. She lived in
India and had worked with the United Nations to help inspire

communities through sport. When the United Nations cut their program, the community saw the value of sports and decided they were going to sacrifice the little money that they had to continue the sports initiative for the kids. Shauna worked another job and volunteered all of her spare time in these communities. I helped Shauna sometimes at these locations and found the communities to be so different from my typical job.

I recall my first day that I helped with the team. As I approached, I heard the players discuss a 13-year-old teammate that had hopped on a train and ran away to Chennai, a town that was a six-hour train ride away, because he was fleeing physical abuse from his family. Another child (age ten) could not attend the session that day because he was working to help feed his family - he would work 15 hours that day. On the other side of the pitch, there was hesitation because a group of teens were waiting to cause a ruckus and beat up a couple of our players. They were the closest version to an Indian-type gang I had seen, and it made my blood curl. This was a very different outlook from my typical Bangalore experience.

Despite all the external distraction and obstacles, the players were driven, intelligent, and grateful for the opportunity to play. Shauna taught these players lessons of goal setting, perseverance, and leadership. The impact of football in the community was incredible. Working with these players was a project slightly outside of the realm of my immediate job, but later overflowed into my actual workspace. In your organization, projects with community involvement are a powerful way to build connections, invest in others, and grow beyond your internal focus.

You can also create opportunities for ownership within projects that reiterate your team values and vision. In India, this meant helping student-athletes create pathways for a future in sport. Many of our players desired a future at an American or Canadian university. My boss and I would put on little conferences and events to share information about university life and opportunities through sport.

The first conference we conducted was comical. I was on holiday in my most favorite state, Kerala, when we first discussed the idea of an event. Kerala is known as "God's own country" and is lavished with unrelenting beauty. Kerala has boundless lush green hills filled with decadent chocolate, tea, and coffee plantations. I often made myself sick from too much chocolate on these trips but I never regretted it.

While relaxing in the secluded hill stations of Kerala, I was surprised that my patchy reception allowed a phone call from my boss. He said that he spoke with a school and they wanted to do a little event to discuss American and Canadian collegiate athletic opportunities. He wanted to know if I would be the keynote speaker. "That's a great idea!" I exclaimed, "When did you want to have this event?"

"Tomorrow. Can you take a sleeper bus and get back up here by then?" my boss replied.

I went back to the treehouse where I was staying and packed my things. I wrote a two-hour presentation, created a slide deck, and made it back to Bangalore just in time. Given that the event was planned in such a short time frame, I was expecting 10-12 people in attendance. I walked in the room and found more than 100 people with notebooks and pencils eagerly awaiting the presentation.

I went up to the front of the room, plugged in the laptop, and all the power went out. The sun was shining so we opened a few windows to allow natural light to illuminate the room. I gave my entire presentation in this setting and I counted my blessings for having a naturally loud voice, considering I didn't have a functioning microphone.

I spoke about different opportunities to be involved in sports at American and Canadian universities from fanatics to intramurals to Division I. I briefly explained different divisions and conferences, the process of getting recruited, and ways to prepare for university sports. I shared the importance of academics, character, and opportunities through sport. I smiled as I thought of the opportunities through sport that shaped my personal testimony in India.

At the end of the presentation, I opened the floor for questioning. The first question I received was, "Is chess considered a NCAA sport?"

Second question: What about table tennis?

Although we had a long way to go, we were making progress in understanding the possibilities brought with sport. We did a series of these events and I continuously speak to student athletes that desire to play at the next level or be involved in sport as a career option today.

In your organization, seek projects that reiterate your vision. For example, if your company has a vision of easy access to education - what projects are you actively doing today to increase access to education? If your organization has a goal of a more healthy community - what projects are you actively doing today to improve the health of your community? Projects are your opportunity to take ownership of action inspired by your *why* and *what*.

Micro and Mega Projects in Teams

Back on the pitch, we continuously found new ways to own projects within our team. Sometimes, it can be difficult to think of a seamless match of football containing room for projects. In corporations, day-to-day operations could also be challenging to identify "projects".

We framed a football match as a single project and a series of smaller projects simultaneously. In football, we framed each player paired against another player as an opportunity for a micro project. The players would engage in small battles for the football to win the match. Every rebound, pass, and air ball were individual projects and opportunities for excellence.

Within companies, framing every customer interaction, each line of code, each transaction, or each data entry as a mini project within itself can be a simple way to reframe projects in corporations. We embraced the mini projects in our team and used them to continue to build momentum in confidence, ability, and ownership.

While some mini projects are ongoing throughout the match, other projects such as set pieces could be seen as mega opportunities/projects. A set-piece is a specific play in football that begins at a standstill as a result of a penalty/foul or the ball going out of bounds. Set-pieces are very special because they are the only times that one team has uncontested possession of the football which dramatically increases the possibility of a score. A set-piece can come from a corner kick, a free kick from a penalty, a goal kick, or a throw-in.

Some teams practice obsessively over perfected set pieces. The German national football team is widely known for their intense focus on set-pieces. In fact, the 2014 German men's team averaged one set-piece goal per game in their journey to become the FIFA World Cup champions. (FIFA)

Set-pieces are a project in which many teams can set themselves apart to establish competitive advantage. Our teams worked on set-pieces tremendously so we could take advantage of the opportunities in matches. We focused on effectiveness for each set-piece in goal kicks, corner kicks, throw-ins, and free kicks to be effective in our play. While corporate teams probably don't have "set-pieces," all have the opportunity to partake in high stakes/high reward opportunities.

The appeal of mega projects or mega events are exemplified throughout our everyday lives. We see this appeal in teams and organizations. We see this appeal in cities and countries. Mega projects are truly Instagram-worthy occasions. You will probably get more "likes" from running the marathon than your daily jog and healthy diet. Your nonprofit will probably get more hype from a large scale free 2,000 backpack, shoes, haircuts, and bicycles give-away than a routine one-on-one school tutoring. A city will probably get more media attention from hosting a FIFA World Cup match than investing in local sports development.

I'm not implying that any of these actions are bad. I've run a marathon, I've participated in nonprofit days of service, I've been to a World Cup match. I also jog every day, I participate in routine tutoring, and I coach at a local level.

Team projects can help define the culture of an organization. We spent a lot of time preparing to take advantage of mega project set-piece opportunities. Our focus on set-pieces contributed to the personality and style of our team. However, football is more than a series of set-pieces. It was our preparation and small wins in the flow of regular play that put us in a position to take advantage of these set-piece opportunities. Mega initiatives are most effective if complimented by a series of small initiatives.

Dare I say, most mega initiatives are failures without a series of small initiatives. You might not get as much recognition from your daily jog than a marathon, but your marathon is less likely to be a success without the daily jog.

Mega projects or mega events can be fantastic additives if the proper work is done upfront to prepare the event for optimistic possibilities. Sometimes teams take on overly ambitious massive undertakings which can result in a frustrated, over-whelmed, and bruised team. Here, the team underestimates the scope and overestimates their confidence. In these situations, projects generally own the team more than teams owning the projects.

Our players were able to take advantage of the unique opportunities within set-pieces that were earned through technical and tactical skill displayed during the course of regular play. The lessons of mega, micro, and everyday projects revealed ways that we could be uniquely better in our style of play.

I continued to give team ownership of smaller projects to build confidence, cohesion, and ability to build up to ownership of larger projects. These projects continued to move beyond set-pieces, position advancement, and clean-up projects.

I split one of my youngest teams into two groups for an end-of-session scrimmage. I gave the groups a 30-second project to come up with the most epic team name ever. Often overlooked, I believe there is great power and success which comes from truly epic team names. What a person and a team are called is extremely powerful. In India, many of the major cities changed their name after independence from their colonial names to their original names. This is why two names may be found when looking at a map or referencing geography in India. Bombay and Mumbai are the same place. Chennai and Madras are the same place. Bangalore and Bengaluru are the same place. The difference in name is a source of pride for some Indian people because they recognize the importance of an owned name.

After 30 seconds, I asked one group for their epic team's name and one team replied they were going to be the Red Fiery Flames and they were going to scorch the other team. At this, they pounded their chest covered by red target jerseys and roared. In friendly banter and smack talk, I chuckled at their team pride and confidence.

I asked the other team for their epic team name. They looked at the intimidating Red Fiery Flames and thought about their team's name. In a moment, little six-year-old Dev went to the sideline and picked up the blue target jerseys and instructed his team to put them on. He looked the other team straight in the eye and declared, "You might be the Red Fiery Flames, but you won't scorch us today. We are the Blue Wet Waves and we are going to extinguish you!"

Dev's little team brightened up and began to cheer. We began a fun scrimmage in which the players competed with heart. Sometimes, powerful collaborative ownership can begin with a collaboratively owned, epic team name.

Generally, an effective cultural shift towards ownership doesn't come from a big announcement or massive sudden change, it comes from small wins building up confidence, ability, and trust. From everyday operational projects, small projects, or massive undertakings, the focus of the players was on their ownership in the success rather than the coach's direction. In your team you can increase opportunities for ownership to be uniquely better by taking on mega and micro projects. For projects big and small, ask these questions of your organization, "What projects could help reiterate our organizational values?", "What projects can we do to help invest in our community?", and "What projects can we do to enhance our team collaboration?"

At the academies, our players were initiating larger undertakings in grander projects through tournaments, skill challenges, and progressions. But our ownership journey was not yet over, as we were discovering more opportunities to be uniquely better.

Chapter Eight
Ownership of Roles

Competitive advantage begins with people. Perfect processes, methods, and projects without the right players would not be successful. Having the right people is crucial.

However, sometimes organizations focus only on the people and hire incredible talent then place them in a system that does not allow them to thrive. The people, the talent, are amazing and have a drive to make things better but the processes, methods, systems, and projects do not allow them to truly excel. To create a uniquely better environment you must look at both the people and the systems under which people operate. We were developing our systems in tandem with developing the extraordinary talent within the teams. In our teams, we had the opportunity to take ownership of our role to be uniquely better.

Roles are not necessarily positions. Many of my players' greatest contributions to the team did not lie in their positional responsibility. Some were encouragers, others were gatekeepers, some were the questioners, some were fast, some were technical, some were the role models, others were the jokesters, and others played the role of lovably obnoxious. In reality, a position is marginal compared to the actual impact that an *owned role* has on the team.

I coached a young 14-year-old player named Praketh. I loved coaching Praketh. I'll admit, he was noticeably physically awkward on the pitch and was not our star player. Somehow, that didn't seem to matter because Preketh had the best game understanding of everyone on the team and played a vital role in helping the team thrive.

He soaked in the lessons that I taught so well that he could personally teach to others. He encouraged and led the team in an unlikely manner. Genuinely kind and gracious to all, he immediately brought a sense of community and family to the team.

One thing was undeniable about Praketh: he had a passionate love for football. His eyes lit up as he entered the pitch. He took ownership of his team and led them in the activities even if he struggled to perform them himself. Praketh loved football so much he would encourage and guide his teammates to the point that I often reminded him that he was not a spectator cheering on the team but actually a vital player. Praketh loved every aspect of the game of football.

Praketh played with enthusiasm and extremely contagious passion. I knew if I was coaching a team with Praketh, his energy would permeate throughout the pitch. Praketh's position of footballer paled in comparison to the value he brought to the team as his own role of encouraging player, team leader, and enthusiastic co-coach.

For some people, an occupational position has very, very little to do with their role in society, role in the organization, or the role in their legacy. Some players own their positional role while others own their personal role.

I thought back to when I was in my corporate life. I had worked in a high stress, large corporate company. The place was filled with white walls, suits, and mainly closed doors. In the midst of it all, there was a secretary who broke the mold. A woman, whom I'll call Sally, decorated her little workspace with pictures of family and friends, filled every nook and cranny with motivational and inspirational quotes, and always walked with a joyfully hummed song and contagious smile. Sally was the joy of the department, a trustworthy friend to all, and a breath of fresh air in a paper-pushing environment.

Years later when Sally left the company, there were few mentions of her position as an excellent secretary. No, her role in the company went far beyond her position. The void was in the former bright little corner of the office lavished with a song and smile. The role a person, a team, a company has in a community is far beyond a position.

The role Sally had was her strength of positivity and relationships.

I have been privileged to work with people whose strengths lie in extraordinary skills such as comedy, leadership, influence, creativity, responsibility, dependability, and outspokenness. Hardly any of these strengths are ever on a job description. But they are the personality which makes you, you.

Praketh might surprise me and become a massive football star one day. Perhaps he will get a better coach who can train him in skill and technique. It's certainly possible. There are a lot of better coaches. I wish this for Praketh. However, I think Praketh *probably* is not going to have the role of a superstar athlete and number one striker on a team. However, he probably will be a coach, a fan, and a major contributor to the game throughout his life. I supported Praketh in his *position* as an athlete while I also championed him in his critical *role* as a team player.

Outside of personal roles, there is also opportunity for ownership within a team role. Personal role ownership is individual. Team ownership focuses on the competitive advantage and uniquely better aspects of a team or department.

After a few sessions of working with Shauna and her players in the underserved communities, I spoke with our leadership team and we decided to sponsor a few of the players to train at our academies. These players would have the opportunity to play on a turf pitch with new footballs for the first time.

We sent the players letters congratulating them for earning a sponsorship. Shauna caught these moments on video as players opened their letters and began dancing and crying and shouting in celebration. It was truly heartwarming. At the time, I simply thought we were doing something nice for these well-deserving, hard-working, and talented players. Turns out, these players did more for our academy than we could ever do for them.

The players came to the pitch and transformed the dynamic of our team for the better. They had a drive and a passion which could not be taught. They pushed the rest of the players to an intensity of training and desire to play that was eye-opening. Our academy teams that had sponsored players transformed into a uniquely better dynamic than the others because they had an ignited drive. Our teams were uniquely better because our teams were made up of a wider variety of players.

The teams that had a diverse makeup that included sponsored players were challenged to greater depths. This was very significant, considering the dynamic of extreme economic wealth of some of our traditional academy players. When sponsored players who had significantly less resources beat traditional academy players consistently to the ball and exemplified respect towards all, it was a beautiful wake up call. The sponsored players redefined ambition and inspired the entire team to dedicate towards more.

The competition was fierce. The more diverse teams redefined their role within the academy as the most driven, determined, and dedicated. Other academy teams took ownership in being the most creative and innovative, the most focused, the most physically strong, the most technically skilled, or the most tactically knowledgeable. Knowing our strength and owning our abilities was critical in utilizing the uniquely better aspects of our team.

Corporate teams can also own roles to be uniquely better. A team could be the "takes-on-great-challenges" team, the most technically knowledgeable team, the smile culture team, the customer service team, the innovative team, the relationship team, the analytical team, just to name a few.

Sometimes, the ownership of the team or department can come from the function of the team. A security team by definition takes ownership of the security of other patrons. In this scenario, go a step further and ask, "How do we specifically take ownership of the security of our patrons? What makes us different from the rest?"

In what way is your team unique? What makes your department or team specifically better? What is a unique quality you can bring to the organization? As a team, own the role you play in the organization.

The opportunities for role ownership didn't stop with personal roles and team roles, we also owned our *organizational* role in our community.

When I first arrived at the academy, a lot of people wanted to learn to play football for different reasons. Some wanted to become professionals while others simply wanted to have fun. Our vision and our focus helped our organization to define our role as the academy who equipped players for success on and off the field. We didn't solely focus on becoming professional athletes at all cost (There were academies who encouraged intense focus on the professional prize above all else. Our academy did not do that.) We also didn't solely focus on fun and learning the game (There were academies who encouraged a good time above all else but didn't have a lot of intensity to the training.

Our academy did not do that.) Our academy was unique in our niche. There were a lot of football academies, but our organization owned our role within the industry.

From personal role ownership like Praketh, to department or team role ownership like the teams with the sponsored players, to organizations that own their role in the community - opportunities for role ownership are an opportunity to establish a powerful competitive advantage. In your team you can establish competitive advantage by providing opportunities for ownership in your roles of individual, team, and organizational impact. What role will you play as a contributor to the team? What role will your team play as a contributor to the organization? What role does your organization play as a contributor to the community?

Chapter Nine
Monkey Business

Meanwhile, other challenges and little facets of Indian life were becoming a strange norm. Some countries have squirrels and chipmunks scattered about their surroundings, we had a wide array of other animals.

Cows, goats, lizards, and other creatures roamed the open bustling city streets without bother. Large insects and bugs were a norm. One day, I was bit in the face by one of these insects which resulted in the left side of my face becoming temporarily paralyzed and droopy with a permanent scar. Another day, I was coaching in a more remote location and my players came up to me and casually said, "MissAmberMam, there is a cobra in the brush over there." I thought they were joking. Sure enough, there was a serpent.

Chris and I took a train to a city called Mysore and went to a marvelous zoological park which had facts about the animals on wooden boards cited by Wikipedia. A personal favorite sign read, "Please be safe. Do not stand, sit, climb, or lean on zoo barriers. If you fall, animals could eat you and it might make them sick. Please co-operate. Offenders will be punished."

At one point, we were meandering through an exhibit for monkeys. I chuckled as I noticed one monkey was inside of the cage and another monkey, who was the same breed, was directly on top of the cage in a tree.

Monkeys were commonplace and commonly a nuisance. Food vendors loathed them because they would steal food and cause a ruckus. One time, I was changing my clothes to hop into a natural pool at the bottom of a double waterfall in Goa and a monkey jumped into my changing area and took some of my undergarments.

I woke up one morning to some loud banging and shouting in the flat. I wondered what all the ruckus was. I heard some screeching and yelling. I got up and went out into the hall and heard the sounds of a monkey. Yes, a monkey had gotten into the flats and were causing all sorts of havoc.

I was warned about sitting with the car windows down because the monkeys could hop into the car. I was in the car one time and a monkey attempted to hop into the vehicle with us. Luckily, the window was only cracked and the monkey was unsuccessful.

The challenges on the pitch, partnered with these challenges of everyday life kept me on my toes in a never-ending learning curve. If anything, the monkeys taught me to embrace the unexpected. As we were transitioning from command-obey to collaborative ownership, there were a slew of unexpected and challenging situations that I faced.

These minor challenges faced in my personal life of monkeys, cobras and bugs prepared me for the challenges I was preparing to encounter in my professional life. Conversations and challenges in transitioning from command-obey really pushed me to examine my ability to lead and overcome obstacles. Transforming from command-obey to collaborative ownership may not have led to challenges like face bites and stolen underwear, but sometimes it felt an awful lot like monkey business.

Part III
Challenges with Ownership Culture

Chapter Ten
Conflict Challenges with Ownership Culture

Transforming from a command-obey dynamic to one of ownership is rarely easy nor smooth. I wish I could write that we changed our training dynamic, everyone thanked us for the ownership, we shook hands, and went on our way. But in introducing ownership, we also introduced a battalion of other challenges which made me question my leadership and guidance into this approach.

It was difficult. Collaborative ownership still has a framework, structure, and projected outcomes. The difference is the flexibility within the framework. The framework moves from acting as handcuffs, to handrails.

There were days I was off balance on one side of the pendulum or the other. I would reflect after some sessions and think, "I could have stepped in more today and more firmly driven progress towards the performance expectations." Other times I would reflect on a session and think, "I could have stepped back more today and allowed the team to lead themselves." There is a balance of when to step forward and when to step back; I was finding my balance everyday as the leader.

While I was seeking a balance as a coach, the players were experiencing more conflict than before. From challenges like the cone - kicking game, I witnessed one of the most heated debates I'd ever seen among seven-year-olds trying to decide if the best way to kick the ball for power and precision was with their in-foot or with their laces. The argument was that one method had more power while the other had more precision. The dilemma was heated and each had their reasoning for defending their method of kicks. They turned to me for the ultimate answer. Which was the best method of kicking? In reality, both methods of kicking the ball were correct.

This is the most unsatisfactory answer but it was the truth. From their dialogue, they now had discovered TWO ways to kick the ball to reach the goal rather than the one single way. Each of them tried each other's method of kicking and decided the preferred method would depend on the scenario in the game.

While the players were able to improve in their understanding, innovation, and game application, this story highlights a new challenge brought about in collaboratively owned teams. In a command-obey dynamic there is generally very little conflict in the *how*. There is one way to do things and it's final. However, when team members are encouraged to use their voice, create an individual approach, or unlock their personal genius, there is a significantly greater chance that these ideas will be different from one another and can spark conflict.

In the team, this naturally felt like it exposed something wrong. With an ownership culture, the team now felt more tension among teammates. They disagreed more. They fought more. With my youngest teams (and teams too old to admit), I had players run up and shout, "MissAmberMam, Miss Amber! He's not doing it the way I do it! Tell him I am right!" I had to teach my players not only how to play football, but also how to engage in disagreement and work together with other footballers.

The team hated the conflict and honestly preferred to be told what to do in an effort to avoid any conflict situation. Conflict was uncomfortable and uneasy. I worked with my players to teach basic conflict management skills beginning with the idea that conflict is not a battle and there is not always a winner - as exemplified in the "how to kick the ball with power and precision" debate.

Rather than, "MissAmberMam! Tell him (or her) that I'm right!" I would encourage my players to engage in the conversation on their own rather than use me as a go-between. I would step in when needed but they were teammates and they had to learn how to work together.

With an opportunity for ownership comes a greater opportunity for conflict-which also comes an opportunity for conversation over complacency. We were challenging norms.

Another lesson for our teams included engaging in proactive conversations. In corporate teams, I use proactive conversations whenever I come into a new team, work on a new project, or begin work with a new client.

Proactive conversations look a little something like this:

"At some point in this project, I will frustrate you. At some point in this relationship, there will be tension. At some point in this team, there will be conflict. It is going to happen. So, while the emotions are low now, let us proactively discuss how we want to handle those situations."

So often we avoid conflict because we do not want to admit there is a problem within the team. Proactive conversations recognize conflict and by normalizing conflict, it provides more freedom to speak openly about areas of frustration and tension within a team.

Many people avoid bringing up tension and conflict because there is a sense of ambiguity about the process and outcome of a conversation. With a proactive conversation, a game plan is created with a script to lay a foundation for some sort of predictability.

The solution may be different in every team. I worked with one corporate team that acknowledged a trend of engaging in circular conversations without a solution. The team agreed that when this became counterproductive, they would timebox discussion then at the end of the timer someone would say the word "ELMO!" as a trigger to make a decision. This acronym stood for "Enough, let's move on."

Our teams would proactively create a game plan identifying the triggers of tension/conflict, an expectation for bringing up the conflict, and a game plan for how to move forward. The proactive conversation laid the groundwork for us to move forward more productively in the future.

Players became more comfortable in engaging in these conversations with their team members over time. The discussions stopped feeling like conflict and started feeling more like normal conversations. Of course, this did not happen overnight, but with patience, practice, and time, these challenges slowly began to see victories.

Saturday morning in Cubbon Park - my favorite park in Bangalore.

Chapter Eleven
Opportunity for Ownership and Challenges in Quality Control

I was in a meeting with all of our coaches and we were discussing the essentials we wanted to teach our players in the upcoming quarter. We were rethinking our curriculum development. At one point, a coach said, "Well, obviously it's not like we can have our kids going around kicking the ball with their toes. We have to teach them how to kick."

At this, Chris shrugged his shoulders and replied, "Why?"

The room went deathly silent. It reminded me of one of those high school cafeteria scenes in an 80s movie right before a food fight breaks out. Everyone looked at the British coach in disbelief. Chris is a very respected and admired coach. I gave a big smile and waited patiently for him to continue.

Chris replied, "If the player is kicking with his toes, let him. We will teach him other forms of kicking to give him different resources but if he wants to kick with his toes, let him. Think of how many goals have been scored in the professional leagues with a slight tip of the toe; there's surprisingly quite a bit! Don't limit his methods-instead expand them. If the player finds kicking with his toe is not effective, he will utilize one of the other methods of kicking that we have taught him."

The room went silent. They knew as well as Chris this meant sacrificing a season of quality for a lifetime of understanding.

On the pitch, I did the same as Chris and I did not command my players who were kicking the ball with their toes to stop. I gave them other tools to use in their toolbox. Within a matter of weeks (usually days), typically the players self - adjusted and had ownership of their actions and understanding of why their actions changed. The change came with more understanding but at a cost of efficiency in training.

With these opportunities for ownership, the players had a greater opportunity to try and fail. In application, this was challenging. The players loved the spark when they understood how to complete a challenge but they became frustrated in the journey of discovery.

I had one player who became upset with me for asking him guiding questions instead of telling him the answers in one challenge. He shouted, "You're the coach! Just tell me what to do! You know the exact right way!" I looked at the young lad and told him I was teaching him and he would not learn by me simply giving him the answer. As a leader, I had to be patient and create a safe space for him to learn.

This does not mean to set the team up to fail. I think in some teams there is this strange idea that if we manufacture failure then we will "get it out of the way" and then we can focus on success. That's not how it works. I tried to set the teams up for success and still trained with the intention of success. I guided our teams with approachable and digestible challenges and coached them in their performance.

In our sessions, we did not start by learning a new skill and applying it in the middle of a scrimmage. No, we learned individually, then in a challenge, then in a progression and another progression and also in a scrimmage.

I tried to build momentum from small wins to set our players up for success. However, when players did fail, and they did fail, I tried to encourage players to recognize this as an opportunity. With opportunities for ownership comes greater opportunities for failure, but also an opportunity for wild success. We were building a growth mindset.

In corporate teams, there is also space for teams to try and fail. This can be done through creating actual physical space, by encouraging more risk in smaller low stakes projects, and allowing time. There are some areas of performance where (unless it is an exceptional situation) you generally do not want any risk of failure. A surgeon operating on my mother is not a preferred time to try a new way to operate on a whim. It is the preferred time to try to follow a plan as closely as possible and only make adjustments as necessary. Flying a commercial airplane is not the ideal time to try a new landing process just for fun. Military forces probably should not try a new form of attack spontaneously when going into battle.

All of these areas make use of a designated space to experiment if possible. Surgeons practice by working on cadavers; airline pilots practice in simulators and in planes without commercial passengers; military forces practice in their academies and in training days.

While there was tension and frustration about the failure on the pitch, there was also an opportunity and a freedom to try and to fail and to learn within our training sessions. We practiced failing and how we would handle our emotions, our setbacks, and our actions when failure might come in a match. We would not give up. We would learn, make an adjustment, and move forward. Again, with an opportunity for ownership, comes a greater opportunity for failure, but also comes a greater opportunity to learn and adjust and improve performance.

I realized that when facing failure in a command-obey dynamic, it is common for the commander to be the one tasked with dictating the adjustment and problem solving for a solution. In a command-obey dynamic, if I commanded a task and it was not successful, then it was up to me to come up with a game plan for improvement.

However, in an unsuccessful *owned* task, it is up to the owners to actively make an adjustment for improvement.

I coached an age-seven player that had been kicking the ball with his toes and was becoming really frustrated at his lack of ball control compared to his teammates. Sometimes his kicks would whoosh dramatically far from his intended target. He looked at me one day and stated, "MissAmberMam, fix my kicks." I smiled at the player and asked him a series of questions about what he could do to "fix his kicks." I reminded him of the different tools of kicking he had in his toolbox. I replied, "Show me a laces kick." and then I asked, "Show me an in-foot kick" and so forth. With each kick, the player had more ball control and demonstrated knowledge of the advantages and uses of each method of kicking in a match scenario. The player knew and could perform the various kicking methods with skill.

I responded to the player, "You have a lot of different skills in kicking the ball and you know when and how to use those skills. So how do you think that you can fix your kicks to have more control?" He looked down and had a real lightbulb moment.

"MissAmberMam! I can kick the ball with my in-foot so I can guide the ball in the direction that I want! Is that the right answer?"

I smiled and admitted that it was one way to improve kicks for better ball control. He began jumping up and down and I gave him a high-five. I then asked a couple more questions about other tools and situations where he could improve his kicks. Then, we practiced different types of kicks to improve ball control.

In a command-obey dynamic, I would have simply given the answer "kick the ball like this" rather than ask a series of questions. In ownership, the players were tasked with problem solving. Sometimes, I would guide the players to answers like in this situation. Other times, I would encourage the players to collaborate with their teammates. Sometimes, players would engage in individual problem solving.

We focused on mastering the simple with extreme capability and application know-how. I believed if the players could master five simple ball skills and apply them with confidence and understanding, they could be more powerful than the player who knew 25 skills but did not know their true power and use. We intensely focused on dribbling, pull back, roll over, step over, and triangle. I placed an emphasis on simplified movements done with confidence and understanding.

The quality was lowered in our initial adjustment to ownership but with time the quality exceeded the level of play previously seen in command-obey training.

Chapter Twelve
Opportunities for Ownership and Personal Challenges as an Authority

I wish I could say I was able to handle each of these challenges one at a time but the reality was all challenges hit at once with multiple teams. It was overwhelming. Keep in mind that I was quite the scandal by my mere appearance even without the unconventional coaching.

India is a land of beautiful flowing sarees and lehenga and choli and kurtas... and then there's me running around with blue eyes and blonde hair in a high Barbie ponytail, shorts above the knees, and coaching boys. By appearance alone, I was a spectacle and talk of the town. With this came a few personal challenges.

Especially with my pre-teen/teen boys, I had to be more careful of my verbiage to assume no inappropriate innuendos could be found in my speech. Teaching skills like trapping the ball with my chest, jumping, or physical contact were all taught with great care and alertness to my body movements and verbal language. I was coaching in shorts and a jersey which exposed more skin than what is accustomed in India for women and I stood out like a pigeon in a henhouse.

For the most part, the players and parents embraced this unique dynamic, and many members of the community came and brought friends and family to watch "the female coach." Several players' sisters came and stood at the fence to watch our sessions. Sometimes, I would let them come and play games with us. We had six new girls start to play football in my time as a coach and all brought their mothers, aunts, cousins, and friends to watch.

One day, I was at a football tournament about one hour away from my nearest coaching location, and a man came up to me and inquired if I was *the* female coach. I admitted that I was guilty of his charge. He smiled a huge grin and said, "Wait here," then disappeared into a crowd of people. A few minutes later the man reemerged with his 10-year-old daughter. "This is my daughter. She has heard of you and has wanted to meet you. Can we take your photo?" After we posed for a picture, I had a chance to speak with the girl about her dreams and was able to encourage her to persevere and do her best.

I coached a girl full of spunk named Silla who brought all of her female family members to one of our sessions to meet the female coach. I met aunts, cousins, grandmother, and mother as they greeted me warmly and thanked me for inspiring their daughter. I had the mothers of several boy players thank me for coaching their sons. They told me they were encouraged to see a female leader in their son's lives. I had encouragement and support from many sides of the community. The Indian community was overwhelmingly supportive in many aspects. The weight of being a female coach for boys was a big responsibility and one that I had not even considered in my initial flight to Bangalore.

This being said, there were times I was criticized for being a female. I had a dad tell me he did not like his son being influenced by a woman. I was criticized for my lack of dominant power in my voice saying it demonstrated a lack of authority. Time of the month was cited when I was upset or angry about something. There were times I was explicitly instructed to be silent because it was not a woman's place to speak in some situations.

There was skepticism about my ability to train the boy players. I continued to try my best as a coach, leader, and person. As you can imagine, the challenges outside of the football pitch in terms of being a tall, blonde haired, blue eyed woman were immense.

I had to remind myself that I had a community of people with character, even people who did not know me, that were protective of me, helped me, and kept me safe. Especially with the stares and inappropriate behavior, sometimes it was really easy to feel like I was constantly alone and targeted, but I tried to focus on the people that were there to help me and keep me safe.

All of this was a lot to digest personally but as I looked out onto the pitch, I smiled as I began to see some progress. These players were my reason for being in India. Slowly but surely, players were becoming bolder in their decision making. They understood the application of their skills and saw the entire pitch rather than their specific individual patch of turf. From our tactical training, players were playing with fresh energy and confidence. From technical training, players were focused on mastering a few basic skills rather than having a mediocre grasp of many. From our physical training, players were significantly in better shape and dramatically more coordinated. They looked like athletes. I encouraged my kids to ask me "why?" and never take my words at face value without their understanding. Even with all of the unexpected challenges, I looked out onto the pitch and thought, "This is worth it."

Opportunities for ownership did not bring an easy transition. In fact, my first few months were difficult in changing our paradigm in how we approached football. I second-guessed my ideas, I contemplated my effectiveness, I reexamined my impact as I saw players become frustrated with the newfound freedom.

There is an idea that all people hate being told what to do, but when it is all a person knows, then it isn't always seen as something undesirable. My players initially did not want ownership. They wanted perfection of a single answer, they wanted predictability of command-obey, and they wanted solely my approval.

The growing pains were intense. I wondered if I was simply disillusioned and if we should just have a command-obey dynamic after all. Were these difficulties in transition worth it? I was not completely confident this idea would work, but I had a belief that it might.

Keep in mind, I was coaching multiple teams six days a week. This transition did not occur one time with one team, it was an everyday challenge with multiple teams. I kept on encouraging ownership in our processes, methods, projects, and roles. I tried to refocus success measures from coach feedback to goal accomplishment. I tried to allow opportunities for creativity within my team. I also tried my best to equip my players to navigate the newfound challenges in this environment for learning.

Although each team had frustrations around the same time, this also meant lightbulb moments occurred in a similar timeframe. We acknowledged that opportunities for ownership can bring a greater opportunity for conflict, for failure, and for frustration—but opportunities for ownership also bring a greater opportunity for innovation, engagement, collaboration, understanding, team camaraderie, retention, confidence, growth, competitive advantage, and higher performance.

I took a breath as I looked out on the pitch and saw more and more lightbulb moments occur. This was beginning to work. I spoke more with the parents and players. I listened and addressed frustrations in our transition, I tried my best. I eagerly looked forward to the next few months as the lightbulb moments continued to occur throughout the teams. Even with all of the challenges in the front end, I truly believed this was going to work.

Part IV
The Progress of Ownership Culture

Chapter Thirteen
Ownership Culture to Increase Innovation and Creativity

I was standing in line for a coconut after a long, hot day on the football pitch. The vendor would cut up the coconut with a machete and after I completed the drink he would open up the coconut so I could eat the malai. Malai is a type of cream on the inside shell of some coconuts.

Coconuts are delicious and nutritious, but also incredibly dangerous when falling. I found myself constantly looking up to make sure I wasn't standing under a coconut tree. Injury or death by coconut is not entirely uncommon. I was walking down the street one day, and a coconut fell a few feet in front of me on a parked car and did serious damage. It felt like a bomb had just crashed in front of me and my heart jumped into my throat.

I was talking to some kids in a remote area in Kerala and a mom rushed out of the house and told us to move away from the coconut trees; a few minutes later a coconut fell right where we were standing. Close calls like this help to develop habits of looking up. While coconuts are dangerous when falling, they are delicious to drink.

As I was standing in line for my coconut, a man came up to me and began to speak French. I turned to him and smiled. This happened commonly enough. Some people assumed that I was

European. Furthermore, I was wearing my Paris Saint Germain jersey - a French football club. I complimented the man on his French but admitted my knowledge of the language didn't go far beyond, "Bonjour, je m'appelle Amber." (Hello, I'm Amber.)

The man then lit up in a different kind of excitement. He was sad that he would not be able to show off his French knowledge but was very excited to speak with an American. He had many questions about the United States. He asked if he could buy me lunch and I agreed.

We walked about a half kilometer to a nice restaurant and the man leaned forward in genuinely attentiveness in our conversation as he asked about life in the United States. I took a bite of my food and pondered his questions. I wanted to give thoughtful and fair responses. This was not the last time a stranger would buy me a meal or chai in return for a conversation.

The longer I lived in India, the more I felt like an unintended spokesperson for so many different ideas. Indian sports, women's leadership, and the United States all became a part of my identity in conversation. Whether it be on stage with a microphone, on the football pitch with a crowd at the gate, or in one-on-one conversations on the street; I had to always be prepared for whatever aspects of my life would be highlighted. I was constantly taking lessons from one team, conversation, or experience and applying it to the next. There were many outside factors that influenced my coaching style as I learned how to better relate to the team to improve performance.

On the pitch, players also began to take their experiences and knowledge outside of football and apply them to their personal style of play. Outside experiences influenced our unique approach to football. Players were taking advantage of the ownership they had within the framework to build connections and apply various sources of inspiration and genius for deeper, quality innovation. This is not a new concept, in athletics or otherwise, cross-training and building connections between different worlds has been a source of inspiration and innovation for generations.

Nearly all of the great athletes cross-trained in other sports and activities and attribute the lessons and skills from various activities to their greatest accomplishments.

In 2017, Alex Collins led the National Football League in yards-per-carry. An absolute joy to watch on the field, the young lad passed opponents with astounding grace and poise. How did such a mass of muscle attain this control, quickness, and fluidity? How did he train to be a breakout star in the NFL? More weights? More running? No. The Ravens running back gained his competitive edge from a source no one expected: Irish dancing (CBS). The control Collins learned from Irish dance aided the professional athlete to have control over his body. Collins proclaimed his biggest competitive advantage was Irish dance.

The value of cross-training goes beyond athletics. I knew of a renowned surgeon who claimed that his odd jobs growing up helped him to maintain steady precise hand movements during surgery. I work with a company which has an international relations manager who utilizes his musical talent and love of music history to connect with people all over the world in the universal language. Exposure to new interests, new hobbies, new skills, new environments can all impact the growth and advancement of a primary role. This concept applied to our players on the pitch.

One of my players, Rahit, also played tennis. He was quick to apply his agility and quickness skills from the court to the pitch. His reaction times were fast and his coordination was remarkable. He would apply skills from his tennis lessons to football and vice versa.

A pair of brothers had a first love of cricket and applied their skill of sprints and speed to the game of football to be uniquely better. They had developed their skill slightly differently through cricket and applied it to be an explosive force on the pitch.

I had another player, Yatin, who recognized the pitch as a geometric equation. I taught Yatin space on the pitch as a series of triangles. If you have the ball, expand the triangles and expand the space. If you do not have the ball, decrease opportune space by creating smaller triangles. From this explanation, Yatin was able to use his knowledge of geometry to clearly understand and communicate ideal field positions to his team. He was a real team leader and had a remarkable understanding of the game.

The cross-training experiences and skills partnered with a flexible framework allowed personalized ownership resulting in excited discoveries. I had players enthusiastically shout, "MissAmberMam! Do you know how I figured that out? Let me tell you!" "MissAmberMam? Guess how I did this? Watch, it's so cool! I did this and then…" "MissAmberMam! Look at this new thing that I've been trying! I can use this when…" These conversations simply weren't happening months prior. I smiled and engaged in each of these conversations as a win.

Players were not having these conversations with only me- they were sharing ideas and building upon ideas with their team members. The players were learning how to engage in conversation to improve team performance. This sounds simple, but in a command-obey dynamic the learning conversation was focused on the commander (coach) only. With a refocus, the players continued to learn from each other in our environment of learning.

Collaborative conversations can lead to unlocking creative genius. In my teams, I took a few moments before the start of sessions to talk to my players about their life at school, at home, their other sports, their ambitions, and I tried to tie those ideas into our training. Sometimes, it was players relating their recent lesson on sublimation to ball progression on the pitch; other times it was players relating their ambitions to be an astronaut to their physical training on the pitch; sometimes it was a player applying the communication skills he learned in a leadership class to actually lead his teammates.

As time passed, our players became more creative in the way that they played football. They adapted personal styles of play to increase performance. One session, the players took a lesson on "give and go's" and began creating different sequences. They took a skill and applied it to different areas of the game. The conversation went like this:

Yatin would ask a question like, "How might we use the "give and go" concept to progress the ball forward?"

Tejas would respond, "I think this would work really well in the attacking third. We can use this to bypass a defender and keep possession while moving forward."

Yatin would follow up with a specific scenario like, "So whenever Shreya is playing as a winger and passes you the ball as a center - mid - she can run down the sideline and open herself up for a quick give and go."

Shreya would then add in another insight, "If we do that, it allows the strikers and center mid to position themselves in the goal box. They can be prepared for me to cross it into the goal box for a score."

Tejas might add more applications and say, "A big pass like that could work! I'm curious, depending on the speed of play, if we are in the center third of the pitch we might also consider doing shorter give and goes in this situation. This could increase the quickness and accuracy of the passes while keeping possession."

Yatin would conclude, "Both of these ideas sound like a good use of a give and go - let's try them both out and see how they work!"

They took this idea and began to apply it to the flow of play, set pieces, and in the attacking third. Soon, the players were taking risks and being innovative on the pitch in real time: their creative juices were flowing and their performance showed they were in the true flow state of mind. We were building our competitive edge. Leaders like Praketh, Tejas and Yatin were all helping to lead teams in taking ownership to improve performance as an academy.

Irish dance and American football both require athletic skills; odd jobs and surgery both require detailed steady hands; ball progression and science lessons on sublimation both require critical thinking - they all complement each other in achieving a goal.

Cross-training is important in so many aspects, including breaking up the monotony of routine, expanding knowledge and skills, providing a holistic view, building camaraderie among colleagues, complementing existing skills, building confidence and independence, and encouraging individual thought and creativity. As we took ownership of our performance, we had the liberty to expand our sources of inspiration within our performance.

I continued in conversations with random people from the street, like the guy in line for a coconut, and expanded my own personal outlooks. I sought to draw inspiration within my own coaching from different sources the same way that players were drawing inspiration from different sources for their performance on the pitch. As I learned more about Bollywood, coconuts, and monkeys, I was able to apply these ideas as inspiration to my training. For example, we played games like "falling coconut" as an agility game to move out of the way quickly of the falling coconut. Why? We needed to be agile and quick in game scenarios. These types of challenges were more personal, effective, challenging, and fun!

With an opportunity for ownership, we found more opportunities to expand our performance ability as we leaned into various sources of inspiration, resources, and insight. With command-obey dynamics, teams were great at imitating - but with ownership we had a team with the power to be intimidating.

Drinking coconut water in India

Chapter Fourteen
Retention and Engagement

People desire a sense of belonging. We long for relationships and we long for purpose. We want to be a part of something bigger than ourselves.

How does ownership affect retention?

The basis of all relationships is trust, and ownership requires a massive level of trust. I had to trust my team to improve in ownership rather than in my directive. I had to relinquish my control and trust my team to do the job. If a team member is given ownership, it is a statement from the leadership and organization that there is a level of trust of the team member. Ownership affects retention because trust affects retention.

Other academies were learning the same skills, and likely doing similar activities, but our academies were different in that we had clarity in the application, progression, and individual approach which would heed our competitive advantage. I continued to clarify the *what* and the *why* and allowed opportunities for ownership within the *how*.

Our academies were growing in size and our engagement was increasing as our relationships grew stronger. The new-found community within our team was transformative in our performance on the pitch.

I had a mother come to me after a session one day with tears in her eyes. She explained that her husband had passed and her 8-year-old son had been devastated. He cried every day for months and ached for his dad. He had been with the academy for about a month and the mother said that the transformation had been unbelievable. His eyes lit up again whenever he was on the pitch, he had something to look forward to every week, he loved the community of the team. Our work was changing lives.

Together, we were building a program and building a team that was performing with greater understanding than the others. There was a contagious excitement. It had been months of exhaustingly tense and heated transition, but now we had greater understanding and began to perform with more confidence and ability. We were winning more matches.

I found myself getting more involved in the players' lives outside of football. I attended one of Rahit's tennis matches and cheered him on. I was able to attend one of the school plays (it was all in Hindi and I only understood a fraction of the play, but I had a great time nonetheless). I was invited to the homes of several of my players to meet with the families. Our players were spending more time together outside of sessions and the camaraderie sincerely affected our team performance.

Outside of the pitch, I was also building camaraderie with coaches and program managers. We were more than work colleagues, we were truly friends. One Thursday in November, I woke up to a different type of surprise. My friends, Ryesh and Sanjana texted me and told me that after the day's training sessions we would be going out to dinner, so I needed to look nice. I came home and got gussied up, then Chris, Ryesh, Sanjana and I took a rickshaw to a very fancy restaurant with a red-carpet entrance. I looked at the sign in the front doorway and saw that it read, "American Thanksgiving Dinner Tonight." Ryesh remembered it was my American holiday and even though I could not celebrate with my blood relatives, he figured I could celebrate with my Indian family.

He and Sanjana had made a reservation weeks prior and surprised me with a buffet of turkey, potatoes, and rolls. I was shocked and so excited. I became giddy and skipped like a schoolgirl to our table. As per tradition, we went around the table and shared what we were grateful for that year. Chris was thankful for the turkey, Ryesh was thankful for family, Sanjana was thankful for friends and a buffet of food, and I was thankful for the opportunity to be with amazing, thoughtful people in beautiful India. The community is what made the hard work worth it.

In your team, recognize that with an ownership culture, players don't only own their specific task - they own team success. Teams perform under a new mindset in which team success does not depend solely on commander directive but rather on the actions of the players. Players are in charge of their success and are encouraged to collaborate with others - leading to a more conducive environment for relationships and meaning. Ownership reiterates trust, collaboration, and impacts team engagement.

People want to be a part of something that is bigger than ourselves. We want to be a part of a community that we trust. We want to be a part of a community in which we are trusted. In our academies, we found that our retention was higher, and our engagement was greater when we provided opportunities for ownership. I found my coaching load nearly doubled in this time as we were expanding, and yet still retaining our excellent players. With our new locations and new teams, I more confidently reminded myself that with an opportunity for ownership comes an opportunity to build something that is greater than ourselves.

Chapter Fifteen
Ownership Drives Motivation

One day, a young coach came to me overwhelmed with discouragement. He wanted to make a difference in the academies but found that the teams in these academies were not motivated the same way he and his teams were motivated at his previous academies based in another country. He thought his current team to be simply unmotivated.

People may be motivated differently - but that does not mean they are unmotivated. This coach was highly competitive and motivated to win, but his current team was more motivated by each other's company. Each team was motivated differently. It is not the job of a leader to ask for motivation, it is our job to inspire it. I tried to heed my own advice as I coached my teams in India. I constantly looked for different sources of inspiration within the teams and individual team players. This was not always easy, and I failed many times before I got better.

I would observe and try different ways to inspire the team. I remembered in business teams, I had some team members that were motivated by education, paychecks, relationships...finding the team's motivation didn't always come quickly.

I had one team that I thought was motivated by competitions throughout sessions, but they were actually motivated by a scrimmage match at the end of every session. I made sure to always schedule a notable amount of time for them to play a scrimmage match at the end of the session. I would try in earnest to not cut their scrimmage time short.

I was coaching another team that I rewarded with little chocolates and candies when they performed with excellence at the end of the match. Why? Because during the Hindu holiday of light, "Diwali," I noticed the players get really excited about the sweet treats.

I was with one team that was super data-driven and loved statistics. The entire team would work very hard for statistics on percentage of ball possession, shots on goal, or percentage of pass completion. We framed this data in the viewpoint of ownership and began collecting more statistics for this team so they could own their improvement.

Sometimes motivation efforts were not effective the first time, and that's fine. I coached several different teams and each one was motivated differently. If one motivation method did not work, then I would try something else.

The easiest way to find motivation is to ask the team members what inspires them. Oftentimes, people know what gets them out of bed in the morning. I would ask my players why they wanted to play football. It can be that simple.

One scrappy-haired kid raised his hand and said he wanted to be a professional footballer and professional cricketer. When the other kids began to laugh at him and tell him that he could not be a professional in two sports he looked at them confidently and said, "I know I can be a professional in two sports because I know of a great American man who was a professional basketballer and a professional baseballer *and* he took on a realm of monsters to save the universe. MissAmberMam, do you know this great American man?"

True, team members might even be inspired by Michael Jordan in *Space Jam*. (Pickett, 1996) I would have never known if I did not ask.

Another form of motivation is to be vulnerable and share personal inspiration with others as a leader. A person's story and passions are valuable. I sought to be vulnerable and share my personal passions. Personal inspiration can fiercely ooze and permeate throughout a team. I believe that one way to inspire others is to show your inspired self. I shared my passion to help the players be their best on the pitch and in life.

Finding motivation is all about meeting people where they are presently. If a team was not motivated in one area, I would try to meet them somewhere else. I sought to take ownership of different methods of motivation.

Then, I thought about how ownership could be a motivation factor all within itself.

I spoke to the Michael Jordan fan and we discussed his hero as motivation towards a vision to be a dual professional athlete. That is a great goal! Now, *how* are you going to take ownership to work towards that goal? Whether it be in your processes, methods, projects, or roles; how are you going to take ownership of your actions and attitudes to reach your goal? This framework of conversation created a deep action-focused motivation.

First, we started with why. Why did he want to be a dual professional athlete? Then, we clarified what. Finally, we asked how. What were going to be his processes and methods of preparing his mind and body to be a dual professional athlete? We discussed specific training, diet, and books that he included in his morning routine and afternoon sessions to be uniquely better than other athletes. We discussed specific projects of competitions, challenges, and activities to establish his competitive advantage. We clarified his what and why then made a game plan within the how with specific processes, methods, projects, and roles.

I noticed how the teams became more motivated and outspoken about their motivation as we incorporated more opportunities for individual ownership and collaborative ownership. Our players were more motivated because they felt like they had more ownership in team success. Without ownership, players were along for the ride. With opportunities for ownership, players were in the driver's seat.

What is the motivation to come to sessions when you are tired? What is the motivation to do your best even when you are having a bad day? What is the motivation to run one more sprint when you are already pushed to your limit?

All of the chocolates, social time, and public praise were secondary in impact compared to the transformation of motivation once we allowed more opportunities for ownership in our team success. Without ownership, the motivation tactics felt more transactional. The player would perform well to earn a compliment or reward. With ownership, the player would perform well to drive team success and then we would celebrate the team success with a reward. With ownership, players felt a sense of responsibility and pride in their performance, and were motivated to take action without carrot nor stick.

I continued my conversation with the motivationally perplexed coach and asked several follow up questions to identify the opportunities for ownership that he could provide with his team. Perhaps the coach's team was not super competitive, but we discovered that they really enjoyed each other's company and thrived in a collaborative dynamic. The best way to motivate them was to give them opportunities to collaborate and have time together. More importantly, the worst thing would be to neglect opportunities for social time, as they were motivated by their relationships.

In your team, how can you utilize opportunities for ownership to enhance motivation for great performance? What motivates your team today? How are you cultivating motivation within your team?

Chapter Sixteen
Discover Individual Strengths

After a long day on the hot Indian pitch, I was looking forward to my after-session ice cream cone. I placed my last bag of footballs in the boot of the car and drank my bottle of water. Then, I looked up and saw a mother dragging her son by the ear. They were walking towards me.

The mother calmly explained that her son, a round 10-year-old boy with a distressed and somber look on his face, had been competing in swim for one year and had not won a medal. Obviously, this whole swim thing was not working out. She was going to pull him out of swim and make him play football as a new sport.

I smiled at the mom and then I knelt down to look at the boy. I softly earnestly asked him, "Do you love to swim?"

He looked at the ground. He slowly nodded his head. We could both feel the mother's eyes towering above us. "But I don't win any medals," the boy replied with a slight crackle in his voice.

I took the boy by the hand and we walked a few paces away for a bit of privacy, then I instructed him to look me in the eyes. I smiled at him and again softly asked, "Do you love to swim?"

For a fleeting moment, the boy forgot about his defeat and lit up, "Yes, I love to swim."

In the next moment, the 10-year-old remembered his predicament in passionless defeat. Striving to build on the momentum of the conversation, I asked the boy why he loved to swim. He shared that he loved to fly in the water, he loved to jump off the blocks, and he loved to make a splash. I smiled at the boy and made a few quips about how I also loved to swim and was a summer lifeguard throughout high school and college.

I asked the boy, "Do you love football?" The boy went quiet. I pressed again in a curious tone, "Do you want to play football?" Still no response. I explained some of the fun things we did in football and asked if it were something he would like to do. He continued to look at the ground, ashamed and uninterested. This boy wanted to swim.

I dropped the subject and I spoke a little more with the swimmer. I cracked a few jokes and we became buds. I then pulled his mother aside to talk to her about the other benefits of sport for her son.

How should we encourage non-medalers? Should we encourage our non-medalers at all? What did I explain to the mother?

First, I explained that personal value goes beyond the performance awards and medals. I quoted my mantra to the mother, "one does not study mathematics to win a Nobel Prize in the same regard that one does not practice sport to become a professional athlete. The value of athletics and mathematics goes beyond the main stage." The harsh reality is that less than 1% of all student - athletes become professional athletes. What roles does sports play for the other 99% of student - athletes in personal success?

I explained to the mother that her child was learning valuable lessons such as perseverance, time management, concentration, determination, discipline, teamwork, stress relief, and enjoyment. We talked about social, mental, and physical development within sports. We talked about how her son's love of keeping lap times and measuring his strokes and counting his breaths were all basic arithmetic and calculations that could help in his education and future career goals of becoming an engineer. We spoke about how commitment to passions can inspire us to dream big.

I connected the mother to some of my contacts within the swimming community and encouraged the boy to try a few swimming camps that were taking place during the sweltering summer. This momentarily reminded me of the earned ice cream cone in which I had yet to indulge. I gave the swimmer a high five and waved goodbye to the duo.

As I ate my delicious ice cream (half vanilla, half strawberry), I contemplated how the academies encouraged its mid level players. I thought about the players that were driven, consistent, and dependable but probably were not the ones winning awards and medals. How could I best support those players?

I remembered a discussion years ago with my colleagues about a Harvard Business Review article that read, "Indeed, organizations often create a vicious cycle in which solid performers are secure enough not to ask for feedback so leaders focus on high and low performers who need more attention. As a result, B performers stay off the radar and get fewer job opportunities because they're seldom considered in career-planning meetings when possible promotions are discussed" (DeLong and Vijayaraghavan).

Without genuine encouragement, many B players can begin to feel underappreciated and begin to look towards other teams and organizations. Losing this vital support can be a massive setback for any team. What is the value of mid - level players? How could I best support my mid - level players?

Mid - level players bring a level of consistency, dependability, and predictability to a team that is not always guaranteed by the "star players." First off, a "B player" is not necessarily a second-tier player because of lack of ability or skill (DeLong and Vijayaraghavan). I had one player that was incredibly good at football but was a rockstar at badminton. The player spent a significant amount of time on his badminton game rather than devote all his time or energy to football. We built upon the player's skills and he was a dependable asset on the pitch during matches but he did not devote the time needed to be a star on the pitch. This was perfectly fine. He did a few things really well that added great value to the team. It wasn't a lack of ability but rather a choice to devote the majority of his energy into something else that made him a "B player".

A team member in a business team may have the knowledge, skills, and abilities to be or do more within the company but chooses to spend more time with family, travelling, or perhaps they do not desire the additional stress. A "B team member" may not be the highest performer because of choice, not because of a lack of skill or knowledge. As a leader, it was important that I acknowledge and respect those choices and adjust my leadership style accordingly. I challenged my badminton player to improve and grow as a footballer, but I recognized the boundaries of my coaching with this player because the priorities were different.

Secondly, "B players" are consistent and reliable (DeLong and Vijayaraghavan). Remember Praketh? The player that was passionate about football and mastered game understanding? Praketh may have not been a world class athlete, but Praketh was consistent in his play. Nobody wondered if Praketh was going to have a "super rockstar amazing day" or a "complete bust forgot-to-show-up day". No, Praketh was going to come and play consistently the same way as always. Teammates knew what to expect from Praketh. They knew his strengths and could play with confidence knowing there were clear expectations. A team member that provides consistency creates a firm stability for others to thrive.

I tried to be intentional to invest time and energy into every single one of my players and to be genuine with my encouragement and feedback. I acknowledged the individual strengths of each one of my players. I did a quick "coach check" and literally wrote down everyone's name and elaborated on each team member's strength and unique competitive advantage. What value do they add to the team?

I then asked myself, "Do the players know that I recognize and appreciate this specific value they are adding to the team? Am I encouraging and cultivating their unique skills and talents? Are we utilizing their unique value within the team?"

This was not really a performance review for players but a self-assessment for me as a coach. Do I, as a coach, know my players as well as I should? Do my players know that I recognize and appreciate their strengths?

As a youth coach and leader, I kept these ideas in mind as I encouraged players. A person doesn't need to be in the center of a spotlight to shine.

While I was having these thoughts, I wondered if I was teaching the same lessons to my players. Were we truly seeing the value that each player brought to the team? Were my players seeing the value of each other?

So often we judge the performance of our players by one aspect of their attribution to the team. Do they score a lot of goals? Are they defending every goal? Are they the fastest? We can easily overlook the many values that a team member can bring by having a narrow measure of success.

As a coach, I had a lesson for my players. *Find where you thrive.*

If you love to splash in the water, jump off the blocks, and count your lap splits, then do that. Who knows? That young swimmer may have a breakthrough and become the next Michael Phelps. That young swimmer may also use his passion for engineering and swimming to create the next great breakthrough in sports technology. That swimmer may swim for a few more years then take the lessons from swim and apply them elsewhere. Just because he was not the best in one facet of a passion does not mean he can't thrive in another. Just like myself, I was not the world's best footballer but I used my passion for football to become an Academy coach. Do not let average performance in one area define your value as a team member. Find where you thrive and pursue that.

As a coach, I had a second lesson for my players: *Value others where they thrive.*

Don't limit the metrics in which you measure value. Fellow teammates might not be the fastest, but there may be another area of value in which he/she can lead the team to success. Recognize the strengths of others and support your teammates in building and encouraging those strengths. Individually, our performance weaknesses are exposed. Together, we are stronger and better.

I returned to my flat and found a package from the United States addressed to me. I only received one package from home during my time in India, so this was very exciting. I opened it and found a bag of my mom's homemade cookies and a handwritten card. I was so excited for a taste of home.

My mom may not be a renowned, awarded baker to the rest of the world, but her ability to light up my day with cookies and a message of love speaks volumes. You do not have to be *the* best-you just have to be *your* best. Her impact does not typically get a spotlight or name on a stage, but it gets a special place in my heart and in the hearts of many people in the Tulsa community.

The lessons of value and worth were lessons that I tried in earnest to teach to my players every day.

I thought of the swimmer often as I tried to encourage and support the many strengths, skills, and abilities of my players. I was intentional to recognize and appreciate the value of every team member.

The reality is, a command-obey dynamic would more easily feature a single measure of success and progression. Ownership lends more flexibility for team members to explore individual strengths and success in multiple areas within the clearly defined *what* and *why*.

Especially with "B players", the different opportunities in processes, methods, projects, and roles allow space for a person to take ownership and add unique value to the team. Praketh may not be a star player, but his role as encourager and coach was immensely valuable. A team may not be the best in one area of performance. Focus on excellence in another area within the opportunities for ownership. Identify one area where your team can provide value and identify one area where each team member can add value then cultivate those strengths intentionally to build the performance of your team.

Chapter Seventeen
Self Organizing Teams

S hreya came up to me and said, "MissAmberMam! There is a tournament at such and such place… can we enter and compete?" Another piped up, "MissAmberMam! We are going to stay after the session and practice shooting a little more. Do you want to stay and help?" Tejas continued, "MissAmberMam! I went over to so-and-so's house this weekend, and we played football for two hours working on these skills, watch this!"

I tried to create space for our team members to self organize. Teams that are overwhelmed, overcommitted, and overworked are less likely to self organize around yet another project or goal. Space allows greater opportunity for productivity, wellness, and creativity. The players had space to dream. I sought to give my players the tools and inspiration within a clearly defined framework that had space to self organize and grow.

Parents became more invested as their children became more invested. The parents were becoming more excited to watch lightbulb moments and witness the dramatic improvement in performance.

Players were working together with their teammates to define their roles as the one(s) who would lead end-of-session sprints, encourage new players, and challenge with new skills. Players self-organized as they sought new projects in the forms of tournaments, extra-training, or new development challenge games. They would work together to experiment with new methods or skills to progress on the pitch. They were taking ownership and thriving in all areas to be uniquely better and contribute to our competitive advantage as a team. It was thrilling to be a part of such a great team of people.

Our team members began to self-organize, leading the change initiatives and improvement work on their own. I was not the only voice to say, "We need to improve the quickness of our passes." Rather, I overheard conversations like this:

Rohit said, "I think that we can have faster passes if we communicate more. I noticed that when we are silent, it takes us longer to see where everyone is and what options we have for ball movement."

From there, Silla added, "Yes, let's try to communicate when we are open for a pass."

Praketh offered more insight by saying, "What if we also communicated when another team member is open. So rather than only, 'I'm open', also say something like 'Shreya is open on your left!'"

Rohit added, "Great idea, let's practice that communication during the 3 v 1 exercise."

Conversations like these would happen without my prompting. They were self-organizing to improve. They were asking the right questions and becoming leaders on the pitch.

I was coaching one player named Arnav that had been working extremely hard at improving his play. At first, he didn't understand the lack of command-obey in my coaching style. However, he was trusting in the training. Though he never said anything, I could tell that he longed for me to simply tell him what to do. I never did. I told him *what* to do and *why* that was important. I gave Arnav opportunities for ownership within the *how,* coaching him along the way. In time, he began to understand and perform better with a series of "lightbulb moments".

He was able to apply his technical and tactical knowledge seamlessly within his style of play. He had grown in confidence and ability. One day, he was soaring in performance. I told him that he was really thriving specifically in applying the passing skills to the game lessons and the sequences. I affirmed that his hard work was showing great results. He smiled and looked at the ground and replied, "Yes, ma'am. You did that."

In a command-obey dynamic, the leader is more apt to take all credit for both good and bad performance since they are directing the steps. This is not the case in ownership. I looked at Arnav and said, "No, Arnav. I didn't do that. You did that. YOU did that." He looked up at me almost as if he was surprised. "Me?" he replied.

I explained that he was the one that put forth the effort in the training sessions, practiced post-session, and applied all of these concepts in a game. I didn't do any of that. It was all him.

I didn't think that Arnav ever slouched. But at that moment, he straightened up and seemed to stand several inches taller. He looked me in the eye and smiled. His confidence in his ownership of play shot through the roof. He sprinted off to continue applying his skills to improve as a footballer.

We had laid a foundation and we were now improving with growing momentum. Parents saw the results and were pleased. Players now understood the training environment and embraced the opportunity to grow as a footballer. We had broken the strict lines; we had disbanded the monotonous laps; and we silenced the commanding lectures as our team began to prepare for our next big lesson.

Our team had learned how to make decisions on their own and now it was time to coach the players in making decisions as a team. Our team had been given the freedom to speak but now needed to learn the wisdom to listen. Football is not an individual sport but it does require the understanding and talent of individual people coming together. We *individually* owned our processes, methods, roles, and projects. Now, it was time to increase our *collaborative* ownership in each of these ideas.

We had big bold dreams. If you can achieve your dreams all on your own, then you are probably not dreaming big enough. If we wanted to do something bigger than ourselves, then we had to include more than ourselves. We had increased opportunities for ownership. It was time to focus on *collaborative* ownership within the team.

Part V
Collaboration

Chapter Eighteen
Collaboration

While some of my time was spent in villages and under-served communities, an equally large part of my time was spent on the opposite end of the spectrum at elaborate events and country clubs. As an elite academy, we would go to the professional football stadium for matches with Bengaluru FC with amazing seats. We would also attend the after parties where the BFC team players attended. I met professional athletes and people in the business that worked with teams and athletes on a professional and Olympic level. Bangalore is known for its nightlife and my bedroom alone was within earshot of five different loud nightclubs that were especially prominent on weekends.

I loved the country clubs and fancy parties. Dressing nice and engaging in rich conversation with considerable flair was loads of fun and comfortable. I became accustomed to this life of extravagant events and living in an elaborate style. I appreciated the extremities of my Indian world.

I went to a variety of country clubs but my favorite was the Bangalore Club. Bangalore Club was established during colonization in 1868. The Bangalore Club is the oldest remaining club in the city. It fancies itself to resemble British-style architecture with an elegant feel: baby blue buildings with open courtyards, tennis courts, swimming pools, badminton, squash, and classy entertainment filled the atmosphere. Large walls hide the outside environment, forming a little pocket of serenity. This is, I believe, the most elite club in Bangalore with famous former members including Winston Churchill.

The current waiting list to become a member of the Bangalore Club is 30 years. I knew several people who were members of the club and I had the opportunity to go often for dinners, entertainment, tennis matches, and lunch meetings. I was able to attend an Indian wedding at the Bangalore Club and was taken aback by the beauty of the place. I always felt so posh and sophisticated, and also at home. I loved it. Every second was amazing.

With this aspect of the job, it could sometimes be easy to lose sight of the fact that the next morning I would be in a sweaty jersey and shorts running around with kids. I ate my delicious food, wined and dined with the best, and turned on the charm on these nights that felt like a dream.

The next morning, I would wake up, throw my hair into a ponytail without makeup and face my reality to work towards my real goal. I was not there for fancy events. It was a fun perk and an important networking aspect of the job. However, that was not the main purpose of my job. I was there to train athletes to be their best on and off the pitch. As a team, we sought to keep our purpose and goals front and center in our training. As we provided more opportunities for ownership, our teams were clearer in that purpose.

When we only focus on standing in a line, kicking a ball, and waiting for direction in our sessions, we are likely to lose sight of the application in a game. When we do not understand the purpose behind our actions and behaviors, we can easily lose sight of the purpose behind our vision and goals.

We had redefined the measure of success from gaining the coach's approval to accomplishing the goal. As a result, we had greater understanding and confidence as individual footballers. We refocused from the coach directive towards our individual ability and ownership on the pitch.

It was time to refocus once more.

We had the confidence to speak and now needed the wisdom to listen. We had sparked individual creativity and it was time to ignite the flames of collaborative genius. Through opportunities for ownership, players could make decisions on their own but now we needed to learn how to make decisions together.

I had some players that were okay with the fact that the team lost the game 10-2 because they had scored the two goals. They had done their job and they had succeeded in their role... but we still were losing games. Our team was more creative and innovative, we had higher engagement and better retention, and we were performing at a higher level than ever before.... individually.

The projects did not mesh, the methods had little synchronization, the processes were not fluid, and the roles were not cohesive. We were not a team; we were a group of talented, confident, individual players. We were not a collaborative jazz band forming a melodic tune, we were a group of soloists each playing our own songs, hijacking each other's moment of play, and becoming frustrated with the overwhelming noise.

We talked about the importance of communication on the field. I explained that communication consisted of two important factors: talking and listening. Effective communication is not only speaking, but also active listening.

As I explained this concept, one of my 8-year-old players piped up, "MissAmberMam! I know this song!"

"You know this song?" I replied befuddled, "Can you sing it for me?"

Then, in the best Vanilla Ice voice he could muster, my young Indian lad began to sing, "STOP! Collaborate and LISTEN! Ice is back with a new rendition! Dundundundundundundun Ice Ice Baby....."

While I guffawed at the cross-cultural reference, the lad had a point. Too often we worry about being heard in a noisy world, but not enough about listening in a distracting world. When working with team members; listen.

Individual success meant little on the pitch. We win and lose as a team. It would require the work of everyone to be truly successful. We had to refocus our work from the individual scorecard to the overall scoreboard. We recognized that while we had opportunities for ownership as an individual, we also had opportunities for ownership within the team.

As I taught this lesson to my players, a few of the all-star footballers looked at me quizzically and repeated, "We win and lose as a team. Hmmmmm."

I had one player named Shiv that decided a solution to this dilemma. Shiv was the all-star player and he decided to be the striker, the midfielder, the defender, left, right, forward, back, middle, keeper.... He was going to play all of the positions and run around and succeed in all of the jobs and then the scoreboard would show a win! Shiv certainly was the fastest and had a strong kick, but as he ran ragged, he began to tire quickly, get sloppy with his technical skills, and was never in the right position. It's really difficult to pass to yourself.

In time, Shiv's effort to do the work of everyone resulted in benefitting no one - least of all himself. In some regard this is reverting to a command-obey dynamic because the voices of the team players are once again silenced. Author Andy Stanley will remind us that "If you don't listen to those around you, you will eventually be surrounded by those with nothing to say" (Stanley). You can't do everything yourself.

In some teams there are people that will try to play all the positions. They might succeed in the feat for a very short time, but over a longer period can lead to greater chance of injury, burn out, and focusing on aspects of the game outside of personal expertise. Rather than performing in areas of strength with excellence, the player performs in every area in a mediocre fashion at best.

To truly win as a team, we had to perform as a team. Rather than performing in every area with a mediocre quality, we had to learn and lean on each other's strengths to collaborate for a better performance.

While Shiv may have thought he was doing the team a favor by doing all the work for everyone, he was actually hurting all.

At the same time, team members were also learning what it meant to be a good team player. I was coaching a team of age-14 boys with a brilliant player named Dhruv who was capable of thriving in nearly every position on the pitch. One day during a session, the boys were split into two teams for an end-of-session scrimmage. The team asked Dhruv to be a defender, but Dhruv didn't want to be a defender that day; he wanted to be a striker.

The team compromised that if Dhruv would be a defender for the first half of the scrimmage, then he could be a striker for the second half. As the scrimmage began, Dhruv stood in the defender position with his arms crossed and shouted, "I will not be a defender today!" The opposing team whisked past Dhruv and scored a goal. Dhruv's team was furious with him and said, "Dhruv! We need you to play defender! You are one of our best players and we need you in this position!" In protest, Dhruv continued to stand with his arms crossed and stood unmoved.

The opposing team came by again and ran past Dhruv to score a second goal.

By this time, Dhruv's team was so upset that they yelled, "Dhruv! We want you off this team! We want you off of this field! We would rather play a man down than have someone who is not committed to this team."

Life was rough for Dhruv for a couple of weeks following the charade. The team did not know if they could trust Dhruv. Other team members who thought of pulling a similar stunt did not dare after they saw the rejection that Dhruv earned from lack of teamwork. Very quickly, Dhruv learned the lesson of team dynamics and grew to be one of the more dedicated team players as he regained trust over time. Team pressure taught him a powerful lesson that day.

This episode brought a lot of tension in the team, but the results were extremely long lasting and more powerful than a command-obey response of "Go play defense, Dhruv." Dhruv worked hard to eventually regain the team's trust.

Players continued to learn about teams and teamwork. We continued to practice collaboration and listening to others to achieve team success. We continuously altered our communication to refocus from the scorecard to the scoreboard by discussing performance as a contribution to team success rather than only individual play.

One way that we altered this focus was by altering our measures of formal success. We had scorecards. This was a part of the academy life. Parents and players wanted a performance review of individual success. The players and parents thrived off of the data. Also, these scorecards had an impact on the players ability to move up within the academy - similar to a performance review's influence on a raise, bonus, or promotion within a corporate team.

I spent hours and hours filling out scorecards for my team players. I used these to measure both my performance as a coach and to act as guidelines for player progress.

However, I also included contribution to team success as a major influence to individual scores. How did the player contribute to overall team success? How did the team member respond to team conflict? Did the player help the team rise to challenges? Did the player challenge their teammates to be their best? Did the team member communicate and collaborate with others? Notice this is not necessarily dependent on scoreboard success. The team could still lose matches 10-2 and that wouldn't deeply affect the scorecard, rather these questions are more catered towards player contribution to team growth and progress.

Focus is significantly determined by how you measure success. When success was measured by the coach's approval, focus was on the coach. When success was measured by individual ownership to achieve a goal, focus was on meeting individual goals for a great scorecard. When success is measured by a scoreboard, focus readjusts once more. The definition and metrics of success drive focus and values in teams.

Our coaching staff sat in heated debates as we discussed how we would measure success. How could we create a curriculum that would equip our players to be successful in meeting our performance metrics? Are those success measurements aligned with our values?

After a lovely evening at a country club, I woke up the next morning and threw my hair into a ponytail. Without a clear focus, it is easy to be distracted by the glamorous events. My measure of success in India would not be measured by the fancy outings. It would be measured by the impact I could make in the lives of my players in my time in India. I had to intentionally clarify my focus and my measures of success as a coach.

I encouraged my players to do the same. I challenged our players to listen to their teammates, champion their team in success, and refocus from a scorecard to a scoreboard. Clarify your focus.

Our team had progressed in ownership, now we were progressing in true *collaborative* ownership.

Networking at a Davis Cup match

Chapter Nineteen
Collaboration and Diversity

I recalled a time I was working in a corporation when a colleague asked me why their developers, cybersecurity, and business teams were not collaborating the way that they imagined. My first questions were, "Does anyone know what developers do?" "Do the other departments understand why is cybersecurity important?" "Do the other departments know what value business teams add?" The answer to all these questions was no. Clarity is the starting point of team success. Ambiguity is one of greatest barriers to effective collaboration.

On the football pitch, collaboration came from understanding positional value such as a player in the position of center understanding that a winger can be used for a give-and-go segment, or a striker understanding that a half - back is available for a quick pass-back to open up the pitch. As teams began to understand the positional value and predict where players should be in a sequence, they were able to make quicker decisions in applying their skill in play.

We would get very specific. In sessions, I would occasionally stop and ask the player that had the ball questions such as, "When you are here and you have an opponent on you here, what should be some options to look for to open up the pitch?" I would follow up the questions to the other players, "What are some ways that we can provide support for your teammate?"

The team members would play out these scenarios, and I saw flashes of understanding and revelations.

The more our teams practiced together, the more they anticipated, communicated, and started to play more like a team. Our team members had clarity in their role and how they could support team members in addition to clarity on what to expect from their teammates.

Players had discovered their own personal strengths and areas in which they could provide value. Now, they were intentional in observing, understanding, and encouraging the strengths of their teammates to contribute to overall team success.

I had one player named Akshar, who was incredibly fast. He was a born sprinter who could outrun any opponent. Teammates learned that they could pass him the ball in an open space further down the pitch at a faster pace than other teammates. Akshar played left wing and was a great option for a pass into an open space down field. Players understood his role, his strength and ownership in that role, and how they could use Akshar's role in game play to progress towards the goal.

A right winger, Aditiya, had a strong and accurate cross. Players learned to anticipate his pass with speed and precision from far distances. A striker, Joshua, was a brilliant player in the air. Teammates played air balls to him in confidence that he would work his magic in an airborne state.

Understanding the positional and personal value of each team member allowed players to collaborate with more confidence. The team members knew the value they could add to team success and understood the value that their teammates could add to team success. We continued to increase understanding of how each team member contributes to the overall success of the team.

As our teams grew and we became more diverse, collaboration added a special opportunity to grow not only as footballers, but also as men and women of character. Diversity in teams is critical to organizational success. As I recruited players from various sources, backgrounds, and geographic areas, we affirmed the immense value of different team dynamics to our performance. With all of the worthwhile benefits, teams that are more diverse should also be equipped to overcome collaborative challenges that are not as prevalent in less diverse teams. As we grew, the differences in our team dynamics went beyond personality, skill, and preference.

Demographic diversity brought about some collaboration challenges. While most of our players were more focused on playing football than maintaining the social status quo, the progress of the masses can be sabotaged by the foolishness of a few. When we offered sponsorship opportunities for the players from underserved communities in India, we found that the drive and determination of these few players impacted the energy and motivation of the entire pitch. I later learned that this socioeconomic mix was quite scandalous.

The social hierarchy was easily seen even to my untrained Indian eye. While India has taken strides and continues to improve in the human equality aspect of society, there is a lot of room for improvement as the caste system still has a prevalent role in the community. Even though caste discrimination was officially outlawed in 1950, the practice is still a part of life both in rural and urban areas.

I was surprised at how quickly I learned who belonged in what caste and the expected treatment and communication towards each people group. Even affluent areas had people of less monetary wealth on the street. Inside of my household, I had a driver and a cook/maid. They lived in microscopic living quarters below us in the garage areas and outside.

I realized the reason the parents and players were appalled at my desired tanning in Sweden was because darker skin in India is the result of outside labor - the job of a lower caste. By the simple look of a person's skin, one could generalize a person's background, job, education level, and status with surprising accuracy. One of my girl players came to me concerned one day because all of the training sessions in the summer sun was leading to a darker tan. She told me that she was beginning to look more like "the help" in her home. Surname, certain facial features, and skin complexion all were signs of a person's caste.

While India is progressing in this regard, the vast majority of the people can be stereotyped and given opportunities according to skin tone and physical features. No wonder skin-whitening cream was so popular, and my pasty pale skin was awe-worthy.

Again, we had very few incidents of inappropriate behavior with our players as we emphasized a strong stance of sportsmanship (demographic or not). Most of the players were more concerned about playing quality football than discriminating against teammates.

However, there were some instances that proved to be difficult learning opportunities. We had some pre-teen teams that bullied darker skinned players and made comments to those that they believed were of lesser worth.

We had a zero-tolerance policy on poor sportsmanship and addressed each one of these instances. Players may have been taught stereotypes about people in society, but those ideas would not be tolerated on our pitch.

I went to one tournament at an International School in Bangalore and was struck by the talent and charisma of a young

Japanese player named Hiro. I spoke to him after the tournament, and within a week he was signed up to play with our Academy.

The young Japanese player joined a team of all Indians. For the players, he was a surprisingly diverse addition to the team. Upon arrival, the 12-year-old Indian players began to tease the newcomer with ignorant stereotypes and remarks.

I held my tongue for a very short moment because I knew what would happen next. My scolding would not be nearly as effective as what my new player had up his sleeve. Hiro got the ball and ran circles around them. He had skill and technique like none of the other players had ever seen. In an instant, the Indian players went from teasing the newcomer to fighting for him to be their friend.

Before they were able to get too carried away, I took the time to talk to them about making flash judgements about those different from us. Our academy would not tolerate disrespectful behavior. I allowed Hiro to build his reputation on his own, but I wanted to make certain that the lesson was clear. This manner of stereotypical bullying would not be tolerated on the team.

From different personality types, to caste statuses, to international talent- a recruited diverse team expanded our horizons. We recruited a community in which we could develop, improve, and play great football. The approach of ownership was different with a greater variety of people.

Diversity in teams brought richness and wholeness. It also brought additional challenges and opportunities for growth. As I recruited from wide talent pools, I intentionally worked with my teams to effectively collaborate to improve our team performance. I also worked with our players to be intentional in including others, being respectful, and seeing the value of other team members. We had conversations and discussions about the topic as more and more people from different backgrounds joined our teams and added a new flavor to our style of play. Our collaboration continued to improve performance and our scoreboards began to reflect more victories.

Chapter Twenty
Full Value Contract

Our team had compiled a set of values. Our team's values did not have to be the same as other teams; this was unique to us. Different teams determine values through different methods and processes. Some teams write out different values on Post-it notes and place them on the wall anonymously. Others have an open conversation. Some teams prioritize and gauge importance by creating a spectrum of values.

Different prompts to create a full value contract include:

- What do we value on our team?
- What does our ideal email inbox look like? (What types of messages and conversations are in the inbox?)
- What do we want to be known for?
- If we were described in one word, what would we want that word to be?
- What is non-negotiable in our team?
- What do we not want in our team?

Examples like these help to define the values of our team. This is a perfect opportunity to lead into a proactive conversation about what actions should be expected and how to address the conversation when those values are not being exemplified in the team.

In India, one value that our team had was to "be truthful". Ethics was important to learn to become successful on and off the pitch. As a coach, I created opportunities for our team to learn the values of ethics. I believe that ethical play is a critical value for players to learn.

I was coaching a team that had a lust for loopholes and cheating. They liked winning, but they reveled in winning unfairly and getting away with it. It was becoming a serious issue. I did not want to police training and spend my time trying to catch cheating so I devised a series of challenges and games that had to be completed as a team and clearly had cheating opportunities. In this, the team learned the value of fairness and that by cheating; we cheat ourselves, our coaches, our team, our supporters, our opponents, and the game.

I stated the rule clearly: nobody on the team could cheat. Even if one person broke the rules, the entire team would lose. Why? Because we win and we lose as a team. In this scenario, it was the high-performing players that loved to cheat. This made the challenge even more infuriating for the cheaters because they were extremely capable of completing the tasks fairly.

It was important to address the cheaters in a lesson that would stick. Telling the players cheating was wrong would not be as effective as this cheating lesson session. Also, I knew that if the unethical behavior continued unaddressed for long, the high-performing cheaters would lead the entire team in unethical behavior. I addressed each unethical behavior that I saw but I couldn't catch every single shortcut during training sessions every day. The cheating, lying, and win-at-all-costs mindset needed to be addressed quickly and decisively.

As we started the session, the non-cheating team members learned a valuable lesson about the importance of accountability. It does not matter if you are doing everything right if you have turned a blind eye to the sub-standard unethical behavior of your teammates. Your individual ethical ownership alone will not excuse the unethical behavior of the entire team. In real life, the entire team could lose games due to unethical behavior of other teammates. No, it's not always fair, but it is a reality of life.

A few players were almost in tears after losing three challenges in a row due to cheating. They got mad. They were infuriated. They hated this lesson. Some were trying their best to be ethical but they were learning that this was not always enough. They had to hold their teammates accountable to the standards that had been set by the team.

The cheaters were infuriated that they would complete a challenge and get no praise because they had completed the challenge unethically. Furthermore, they were letting their teammates down. They passionately agreed that cheating wasn't worth it. They chose to play fairly and hold one another accountable for ethical play. They had a proactive conversation about accountability with their team to perform with character. When they finally did win, the celebration of victory was exuberant and flamboyant.

The players didn't outcast the cheaters as I feared might be a byproduct; rather they were challenged to raise the standard of the entire team and hold themselves and others accountable to what was expected of them. When I asked the players about what lesson they learned that day, they wiped away their tears of frustration and shouted out, "When we cheat, we lose! And it is no fun!"

With an opportunity for ownership, team members take ownership of action. This is great! But make sure that the quality, values, and ethics of those actions are in line with the *why* and *what* of your organization. Our players had flexibility within a clear framework but when those actions moved outside of the defined standards - there was a problem. Our team encouraged quality control and accountability within the team. We encouraged innovative problem solving while also reiterating clear standards and values.

This reminded me of so many other business teams that had a few individuals who did not uphold the full value contract and cost the entire team. I was reminded of Volkswagen installing a software to falsely pass emissions tests. Surely every single person in the company did not know of this Environmental Protection Agency regulation sabotage. However, the scandal cost the entire company nearly billions of dollars and a damaged reputation. Everybody in the Volkswagen organization was affected by this breach of value contract. (EPA)

The subjects within a full value contract can go beyond ethics and environmental responsibility. Our teams discussed actions and attitudes towards challenges, teamwork, and communication within our value contract. In every value, we clearly identified *what* the value was and *why* it was important. We also discussed *how* that value would be demonstrated within our team. We discussed *how* we would address a lack of value demonstration. We owned our values individually and collectively in collaborative ownership.

In your organization, I encourage you to ask your team about the values that will guide the actions, attitudes, and behaviors. Identify why those values are important. Share specific stories of how those values are expected to be demonstrated within the context of your team. Agree on the action steps expected

In India, we reiterated our values. We valued ethical behavior and intentionally put that value into practice. We also addressed when the values were not being exemplified to our standards. The team was taking ownership of team performance and the team values.

Chapter Twenty-One
Practice Collaboration with Micro Teams

There were two reasons why a player would desert any practice: rains and exams. Especially during the monsoon season, the rains would clear a session faster than Aerosmith clears a country dance hall. Weather dissuaded players from coming because rain could cause sickness which would lead to absence from school. Sometimes we would show up to the pitch after a one or two-hour drive only to find the rains had left us with zero players to train. The rainy season was a tough time to coach players in India.

As much as I disliked the challenges of the rainy season, I was always glad that it meant the end of the summer season. Our flat, and many places in Bangalore, did not have air conditioning. For decades there was not a major need for air conditioning because Bangalore is the "Garden City of India" and known for moderate weather. Industrial development and hacking of trees have led to dramatic rising heat and unbearable summers. In the summer, three of my players' cleats melted on the hot turf. The air conditioning in our car was not great. Our long commutes rotated from opening the car window hoping to get some breeze in our standstill traffic, to sitting in our sweaty puddles blasting the subpar A/C hoping for a burst of cool air.

Nights were the worst. I had opened screened windows and a single fan on "high" all night. Sometimes, it would get so hot that the power would go off. Everybody in the flat would wake up within minutes of a power outage because it meant the fans were off, and this was significant. It also meant our drinking water filter was inoperable. I was somewhat paranoid about the possible lack of drinking water and had a nightly routine of filling 8-10 glass bottles before bed. One time I had not done this and we ran out of water for a couple hours during one of the outages. I did not want to be in that position again.

With the misery of summer, I welcomed the rainy season. The rains were heavy and intense. It's not a shower, it's a downpour. The height of exam season and the beginning of the rainy season are near one another which led to many sessions containing only a few players throughout this season. During these sessions, I experimented a lot with micro teams. Micro teams are a powerful tool that we used throughout training, regardless of weather, to disrupt and develop our football skills.

In training sessions, I would instruct my players to form teams of three to five that included at least one person who was not on their previous micro team. This allowed the team members to work with different dynamics and helped to steer away from cliques and super groups during practice. These micro teams would be given challenges that would require the contribution of everyone to be successful. The disengagement of even one person would result in challenge failure.

Why practice collaboration with micro teams? Small teams provide an environment for quick-failing learning which leads to innovative and bold disruption. Micro teams resolve possibilities for any individual slacking. Large teams and organizations thrive in developing and improving existing processes, methods, roles, and projects. Smaller micro team's ownership opportunities typically thrive in disruption rather than development.

Small teams can fail at a faster rate and mature at a quicker pace than larger teams. Smaller teams can acquire, adjust, and adapt new skills and information in a more efficient way compared to larger teams. Large teams develop, small teams disrupt. In these micro teams we would disrupt our collaborative behavior. At the end of the session, we would come together as a large team to develop upon the foundation we laid.

In application in our training, we progressed our focus and collaboration accordingly. The focus of our session routine looked like this:

- Warm up activity to get physically and mentally ready (focus on individual ownership and skill towards a goal)
- Activity 1 to introduce or develop a skill or concept starting with a foundation and increasing progressions (focus on expanding and developing individual ownership and skill towards a goal; how does that apply to the team; practice with a micro team)
- Activity 2 to progress and apply the skill or concept in match examples (focus on collaborative ownership towards a goal in a micro team; disrupt the process)
- Scrimmage with a focus on the day's lesson (focus on collaborative ownership towards a goal in a larger team; develop the process)
- Gather for a debrief of the lesson, discuss takeaways, and give two sprints down and back (focus on application of ownership opportunities to larger goals in a match, tournament, or season)

After working on expanding and contracting space within ball movement, I challenged my 16-year-old players to play 3 v

1 (three players versus one player) in a confined area. The players practiced how to expand space to make it more difficult for the one opponent to get the ball. They also saw how less space made it easier for the opponent to get the ball. The natural shape of three players is generally a variation of a triangle, so a general dialogue was about expanding and contracting triangles.

A player named Puja struggled with understanding the use of space on the pitch. We had just completed a series of 3 v 1 in a micro team in which she really excelled. I asked Puja to point out the triangles on the large pitch. It took her a moment, but as she looked thoughtfully around the pitch, I saw a lightbulb come on as she pointed out the myriad of combinations of triangles around the pitch. "Imagine you are playing 3 v 1 except now you have more options and more triangles." It clicked and she totally rocked in ball movement with her fresh understanding. We took our lessons from disruptions in micro teams, and we developed in larger teams.

The concept of micro teams seamlessly flows into corporate teams. Amazon CEO Jeff Bezos is famous for his simple, "two pizza rule." He believes that it is important to limit the number of people in a team to the number of people that could eat two pizzas (Bezos). Two pizzas would probably not satisfy the hunger of 26 people, but it could probably satisfy the hunger of more than two people. Bezos believes in this concept because with a larger group, there is a risk of inhibiting innovation and efficiency. Meet in a micro team to make quick, agile, and creative solutions. Disrupt within ownership opportunities in a micro team. Afterwards, develop ideas and ownership opportunities with the larger group.

You can create an environment for uniquely better performance by inviting the right people to the table. Too many voices and opinions can cloud clarity. Disrupt your processes, methods, projects, and roles in micro teams then develop in larger situations.

The rainy season continued and I looked out the window of my flat and the rains began to pour again. I looked down into the street to find the Scottish and British coaches extremely excited because rain reminded them of home. I saw them standing contently in the downpour, relishing the feeling of normalcy. I loved to see how people from different countries responded to India and what facets of home life they missed. I also chuckled at the aunties giving judgemental looks in the corner towards the guys, convinced they were going to fall ill because of their desired rain exposure. I wondered how this weather would affect the day's session turnout. Either way I was prepared to disrupt with micro teams and develop with large teams.

Chapter Twenty-Two
The Power of Retrospectives in Continuous Improvement

A s our teams improved in collaboration, conflict management, and sportsmanship, I sought to build upon the momentum by teaching my next lesson: the importance of continuous improvement. One powerful tool that we used to improve
performance was retrospectives.

Retrospectives occur at the conclusion of something. In
sports, it is very simple to know when the conclusion occurs
because teams look at the scoreboard when time has run out
and teams have a definite sign of success. Teams know without
a doubt if the goal has been achieved.

In other organizations, this could be the end of a project,
the end of the quarter, end of a season, or end of the week. This
is a time to reflect about what has gone well and how to adjust
moving forward.

In the retrospective phase, it is important to take a moment
and acknowledge the emotion that comes with the conclusion.
Sometimes we celebrate and other times we mourn; either way
it is important to acknowledge the emotion in the moment. I
would not begin talking about continuous improvement immediately after a huge overtime championship win. First, we
would celebrate! Take a moment to process the emotions and
use it as a time for unity within the team.

The second part of retrospectives are preparation for the future. After the celebration or the mourning, we then began to look for opportunities for continuous improvement. "What did we do well? What was confused? What can we do better?"

We had retrospectives often in our teams. At the end of every training session, we would reflect on what we learned, what we did well, and what we could improve for next time. We also conducted a retrospective at the end of our matches, the end of tournaments, and at the end of a quarter. I initially led the team in questions and listened carefully to their answers. Soon, the players were leading their own retrospectives and I acted more as a facilitator. The team was taking ownership of their team performance and I was merely there as a coach to guide and develop.

An experience that goes unexamined is not very effective. Remember, the statement, "We didn't lose, we learned" does not carry much weight without the follow-up question, "What did we learn?" Retrospectives are a powerful conversation to take ownership of team performance.

I encouraged my team to know the purpose behind performance feedback and to get specific to get strategic.

I often heard coaches shout in exuberant fashion, "Good game!" "You're doing awesome!" "Keep up the good work!" While this may sound nice, it is not specific enough for the player to know exactly what behavior is desired to be repeated.

When giving positive feedback, the purpose is to encourage continued desired behavior. Be specific about what behavior should be repeated. What specifically about our performance was great? Bestselling author Andy Stanley is quick to remind us that "if we don't know why something is working when it's working, we won't know how to fix it when it is broken" (Stanley). Specifically calling out the success in certain opportunities for ownership was a really powerful way to reiterate the small wins throughout our team performance. "Good sharp pass!" "Great job staying with your man!" "Awesome communication on that one-two play!"

I also encouraged team members to be specific to be strategic within corrective feedback. I once had a player that was known for coming into the huddle at halftime when we were losing and knew with immense confidence what we needed to do to turn the game around and win. He would smile and state plainly, "Guys, we just have to play better." In this one statement the player seemed to matter-of-factly solve all of our problems. Yes, the answer was technically correct but a little too vague to be of any use.

"How can we play better?" I would ask.

One player would respond, "We can keep possession of the ball more. We keep turning it over to the other team."

I would reply, "Okay, how can we improve our ball possession?"

Another player would point out, "Well, we can make cleaner passes."

I would press once more, "How can we make cleaner passes?"

Finally, a player would pipe up, "Well, if we look up to see our intended pass rather than blindly passing, we would probably make cleaner passes and keep possession of the ball."

Then another would add, "Remember how we talked about our communication on the pitch to let the player know who is open and where to pass? I believe that would help as well! Let's make sure to communicate with our teammates to help them know where to pass."

Through a quick exercise, we were able to turn the statement of "play better" into an action step, or rather a series of actions steps. Players knew to "lift your head and look to see where you are passing the ball" and to "communicate to your team members that have the ball."

I would go through a series of *what* and *why* to formulate specific corrective feedback. What specifically can we do to play better? Asking a series of questions going several layers deep allowed for very specific action-focused feedback.

Finally, in my coaching, I sought to be very specific in building upon performance or teaching new aspects of performance within my team. Vague performance feedback warrants vague performance improvement. Whether encouraging desired behavior, correcting undesired behavior, or coaching behavior, team members were encouraged to get specific in our retrospectives so that we could take ownership in our strategy to improve, develop, and grow.

We knew the purpose of our performance feedback and our retrospectives and we were in the habit of conducting each activity consistently as an intentional act of performance improvement ownership.

As I was guiding my team in retrospectives and collaborative performance improvement discussions, I knew that we were ready to begin a final conversation and mindset shift. We had focused our energy on transforming the command-obey dynamic to one of ownership. We then pivoted to add *collaborative* ownership to our training dynamic. Now, we addressed the transformation of the former commander.

Part VI
Captainship

Chapter Twenty-Three
Defining Captainship

In a comman-obey dynamic, there is an inherited idea that if you obey and obey and obey and obey and obey long enough then one day you will have the opportunity to become the commander. From day one, I had players ask if they could be captain. I agreed that any player could become captain if they could define what a captain was in our academy. From a command-obey mindset, the players would light up as they confidently thought they knew the answer. Countless times I heard the response without variation that a captain is "the person who tells others what to do."

In a bold move, I did something I had never done before on a team. I essentially took away the entire position of a captain for the first few months on the job. We worked around the logistics and figured out how to function without the position. In reality, no players in our teams were yet ready for the job of captain.

The first thing that we did was define captainship. Whether it be Captain America, Captain Underpants, or Captain Crunch; captainship can be defined very differently depending on the organization. Our job was to find a definition that we could collaboratively own.

We decided that a captain in our academy was a person that did the following:

1.) Strove to be their very best every day.
2.) Served the team to be their very best every day.

It's not a great definition, I'll admit it. That wasn't the point. The point was that we actually had a definition of captainship that would reinforce collaborative ownership. We had the right to alter the definition in the future as our team progressed, but this was our current standard that we agreed upon for our captains.

Lessons of *servant* leadership had a different luster in India. We had people who served us in India. We had people that picked up our shoes, did our ironing, drove us places, made us food… and this was not a dynamic of parents and their children. We were surrounded by people who humbled themselves and served us in our homes every day. Servant leadership takes on a different meaning when you see the actual job of serving every day. It's a type of humility that goes way beyond any theoretical knowledge.

A few of the players were outraged by the definition of captainship. They were not upset by the verbiage, but for the lack of power that this definition contained. They were seeking a profound definition that was even greater than "tell other people what to do." I was teaching them that a leader does what we had been doing all along.

"MissAmberMam, I have to listen to these fellows, and I can't tell them what to do! MissAmberMam! I've already been doing that!" one exclaimed.

"MissAmberMam! You mean that now I have to listen and give even *more* to my team than what I am now?! I thought the captains didn't have to do all that!" another disappointedly hollered.

The players did not realize we had been preparing them in the character and skills of a leader from the very beginning. We had been preparing them to take ownership of the role of a leader from the first day on the pitch. I was now placing a name and a new level of intentionality to our expected behavior. We strove to build our role of leaders from the very beginning, and *then* teach the position of captainship- not the other way around.

Naturally, the ones who were so outraged weren't exactly ready to take on the position of a captain. However, there were some players that had been in the role for months and were ready for the position.

In a very short "captainship training lesson," I went over the responsibilities of the *position* of captain such as calling the coin flip at the beginning of the game. I continued to help all the players progress from basic leadership skills. I had confidence in our captains and their *role* of team leader. They had been prepared for some time. Yes, it was important that they knew how to behave during a coin flip or confronting the referee, but it was much more important that they were prepared to lead a team and encourage a team to great performance.

In a command-obey dynamic, a captain is a commander. In a collaborative ownership dynamic, the captain is the leader. In our team, we sought to train our leadership for the character of the role first, then focus on the specifics of the position second.

Chapter Twenty-Four
Leaders Ask Why

I was coaching at an Gameday Summer Camp in the scorching heat of India. While we did not have an age limit for the camp, most of my players were ages 12-14. As we were beginning to start the first day of camp, we heard a loud shout and I followed the player's eyes to discover the source of the noise. It came from a ball-of-energy footballer named Ojas, who was six years old. I heard the players give an audible moan towards the runt and feared for the dynamics of the camp. I prepared myself to adjust and lead in this new team dynamic.

Almost immediately a player named Benedict, who was an incredibly talented footballer, befriended Ojas. Benedict had shown off his talents on the pitch and had distinguished himself as the most capable player in the entire camp with admiration from all. He had confidence, but not an ego. He was easy to train and open to correction and coaching. He had a strong foundation and was eager to fine-tune his skills.

While Benedict could have taken the opportunity to state his dominance on the pitch, Benedict instead refocused towards his new friend. He led the other 30 players in focusing on football improvement and growth as young men and women of character. Benedict understood that this was the opportunity to pour into others on the team. Those who mocked and teased little Ojas were ridiculed for their behavior by Benedict, and soon the culture transformed to one of an individual showcase to one of team improvement and growth.

As a result, the team became more determined to grow, more others-focused, and more improved as players. Ojas became the beloved little brother of the 30 preteen boys. They looked after him and loved to help him. Ojas had a few modifications to his training but overall did his best to keep up with the rest of the team and laughed all the time with joy. He had an entire team of players helping him.

Benedict was humble, hungry, and smart. Benedict embodied the ideal player that I want on my team. Benedict was a leader—a true captain that embodied our definition. Benedict and Ojas became inseparable; they were bonded brothers and great friends. It was truly inspiring. Benedict took time to perform his best, but he also took the much-needed time to help others perform their best also.

The players were beginning to act like captains on their own accord and performance continued to improve. As I was coaching several teams at one time, it was amazing to see the fruits of labor in several team dynamics simultaneously. After months and months of challenging work, we saw creativity, collaboration, and captainship.

The performance was remarkable. The players were inspiring. The parents were pleased. I could not believe that it was all working as I had hoped on that plane ride a year ago from Sweden.

Benedict was not the player who embodied our definition of captainship. Another incredible leader was named Tejas. I first met the player his first week with the Gameday Academy. Tejas had seen the Premier League on television and wanted to give the sport a try. I began to work with Tejas and saw his passion for the sport as more than a short infatuation. Tejas poured his heart into football. He absorbed everything like a sponge and within a few months was running his own personal sessions at home.

I mentioned Tejas earlier as the player that desired to be an astronaut. He channeled all of his energy to improve and learn in a multi-layered, deep-rooted sense of purpose.

Tejas understood not only the technical, but also the tactical side of sport. He was a relatively quiet and reserved person until he began to play on the pitch. He was a quick student and a swift player. Tejas began to develop physically, technically, and mentally as a player.

Within six months, Tejas lost a notable amount of weight from daily exercises. His balance, agility, and coordination was significantly improved. Soon, he was playing with teams 3-4 years his senior. Like Praketh, he was half player, half coach with a firm knowledge of the game. He patiently helped others to improve as players and took the time to build relationships with every teammate. He understood his teammates' strengths and opportunities for growth, in addition to knowledge of his own strengths. He collaborated with the team to exceed goals. Tejas had a servant's heart for the team and a commanding presence on the field.

Stories such as Benedict and Tejas filled my heart, and I knew my time to leave was coming soon. While I did not want to leave my dear adopted country, I knew that my next challenge was waiting for me. Our teams were playing with more confidence, creativity, collaboration, and captainship. The performance improvement was dramatic. Our grassroots programs had exploded, and our elite academies were performing better in tournaments. This had been a long journey. I stood and watched players like Benedict and Tejas with a satisfied grin.

I continued to coach my players and continued to see them play with more confidence applying their mastered skills in matches. We were winning more and progressing quickly. I wondered how the players would respond if they had the opportunity to return to command-obey, would they prefer returning to their old ways?

One session, I had an outside guest as a co-coach who trained his team in a loud command-obey dynamic. He was giving a drill and a couple of players were inquiring about the game application and asking "why?"

The players were persistent in talking about the application and inquiring about the drill in relation to the game scenario. This coach was getting extremely frustrated at the questions and finally looked at one of the players and shouted, "STOP ASKING WHY! THAT IS A STUPID QUESTION!"

The player looked at the coach nervously and began to sheepishly walk away, then he paused and turned around to face the coach again. He timidly replied with overwhelming conviction, "No, Sir. 'Why' is not a stupid question." I beamed with pride as I quietly smiled at the young player.

I made eye contact with the player, and I gave him an affirming nod and smile. Life would tell them to stand in a line and kick a ball without questions, but they had learned that "why?" was not a stupid question. They had learned to see the big picture, to be inquisitive, to seek understanding, to be boldly innovative, fiercely collaborative, and cling to connection.

I respectfully explained to the co-coach that I had taught my players to ask questions, and they were doing as they were trained. The past year had led to this point. I had been criticized early on that my coaching methods were not the most efficient and that it was much faster to simply tell the players what to do. This is true. It is more efficient and less challenging to simply tell others what to do, but it is not as worthwhile and does not lead to championship teams.

Creativity, collaboration, and captainship building can be a messy and worthwhile process. As a coach, I believe that my job is to teach players skills that can be used on and off the field. I believe that, like captainship, it is more of a role than a title. These players not only understood this concept of ownership, but they also felt conviction to stand up for the idea.

The players now had ownership and responsibility to make decisions individually. They had been tasked to use wisdom to listen and collaborate to make decisions collectively, and they gained the confidence and skill to lead the team in decision making environments. We had come a long way, and the journey was only beginning.

Chapter Twenty-Five
Preparing for the Future

I lived next door to the M. Chinnaswamy cricket stadium for the Royal Challengers Bangalore team, and on match days the streets would be filled with people in an Indian version of tailgating. I could hear the loud cheers in the distance and watched the local kids play cricket in the nearby park. I tried to understand the infatuation of cricket but never really grasped the sport. I really enjoyed other popular Indian sports such as kabaddi and field hockey, but have yet to become a passionate cricketer.

I met a friend who was a professional cricket star who sponsored an academy in Chennai. Next thing I knew, I was on a train to the Chennai cricket academy to give coaching lessons to cricketers without much knowledge of what I could teach these athletes. I did not know anything about bowling or hitting so I decided to teach the athletes proper sprinting techniques. That was the only aspect of the game that I felt I could add any value as a coach. After I taught them sprinting techniques, the cricketers tried to teach me how to bowl (kind of like pitching in baseball). I threw the ball far left into a different net. I was horrible, like embarrassingly terrible, and I laughed at my complete failure while gaining new respect in the talent required for the game.

After the training, all of the athletes gathered around me, and I shared a message with the cricketers about choice. Every day they had a decision to make. They could lay in bed and do nothing, have a bad attitude, give a mediocre effort, and waste the day. That is a valid choice that they could make. Or they could decide to give their best, have a good attitude, and be kind to others. Everyday they had a decision to make. It was not a groundbreaking lesson; it was a simple mindset that could change a lot.

However, this simple lesson prompted a cricketer to raise his hand and respond with conviction. "Every day I am going to choose to do my best in school and in cricket. But I am also going to choose every day to be a good big brother to my siblings and set a good example for them. I know they look up to me. I want to be a brother they can be proud of."

I was constantly amazed at the heart of these kids. I was convinced they could do anything. These athletes understood that their biggest impact could be made through a series of everyday choices, a series of small shifts, a series of little improvements.

I thought about my players on the pitch, the changes in communication, ownership, and approach we had made. Like the everyday choices that we make, these were not dramatic changes-but merely slight shifts that made a big difference. Sometimes the biggest changes come from the smallest of shifts.

I returned to Bangalore and sought to build on our momentum as an academy. I worked with our program managers and coaches to establish some sort of knowledge management. Beforehand, every coach would create sessions individually and we did not have any sort of knowledge-sharing process. As I prepared to leave, I wanted to help create some way to capture the knowledge and ideas from other coaches so that knowledge would not be lost when coaches left, and incoming coaches could have an easier onboarding process with the content, ideas, challenges, and triumphs.

From a series of failed organizational initiatives, I knew even the greatest processes on paper would be useless if it wasn't practical for the team. We had tried different equipment management processes that looked great on paper but were a disaster in the implementation because they didn't account for the hectic moments of cleaning up, changing locations, and dealing with different team sizes that required equipment bundles to be continuously altered and adjusted.

Our coaches were not yet at a place to create sessions online. Some did not have a computer or laptop. We printed paper session planning templates for coaches, then categorized them in a Penda-flex for easy access. Categories included training sessions like attacking, defending, and shooting. It also included slots for tournament logistics, common Q&A, and learning moments. I took a picture of each session and document, and included it in a very basic online Knowledge Management System in case the Penda-flex got lost. This also provided a foundation for when an online Knowledge Management Systems would be more practical and more widely used. One of the program managers also began to take on the task of online knowledge management and agreed to continue the responsibility when I left. We did not need a massive Knowledge Management System software; we just needed a practical usable process like a paper Penda-flex to lay the foundation for future knowledge management.

I also created an in-depth onboarding process for incoming coaches and staff. I believed that one reason for the coach turnover was unmet expectations and lack of preparation. I created a month-long onboarding process that included a directory with our staff and contact information, our coaching philosophy and academy approach. I outlined timelines for training and included keys to success in the job. This also included things that are not in a general onboarding process for our international coaches such as places to eat in the area, nearby medical facilities, and slight quirks about living in India. I hoped that this would improve the transition for talent as the organization continued to grow and expand.

We began to partner with other academies and international talent which resulted in more matches, and we set the stage for a legitimate league moving forward. This would become more of a conversation and more legitimate after my time. I was so excited for the future of Indian sports.

Through Gameday Academy, we helped to organize a massive city-wide event called Adidas Uprising. This was a humongous two-day event that included tens of thousands of people involved in athletics, aqua workouts, badminton, basketball, cricket, cycling, phantom workout, rugby, running, tennis, volleyball, wall climbing, and even yoga and zumba, in addition to football. The energy was contagious, and our players were so excited to compete with the best for the coveted Adidas Uprising trophies.

In tournaments like these we played well as a team. We played *extremely* well. It felt like a different team than last year.

Enjoying a match the Bengaluru FC stadium

Chapter Twenty-Six
Connected Collaborative Ownership and the Future of Indian Sport

As I work with the development of international sport, I hear various conversations about emerging nascent national teams like India progressing in performance more quickly than established national teams like England. India is making up for lost time and catching up comparatively quickly in terms of basic football resources, technology, and curriculum. This is a very similar idea to a macro-economic idea called economic convergence theory.

Within this multifaceted theory, it states one of the reasons that emerging countries progress faster than established countries is because they can use the technologies and lessons from previous countries to lay their foundation for growth.

Established countries spend energy discovering the "new" while emerging countries generally spend energy learning from established countries as their predecessors and avoid any repeat mistakes as they play "catch-up". While this theory is oftentimes related to macroeconomics, I believe that it can also be applied to sports teams.

However, there is a catch to economic convergence theory. While a country (or organization or team) may develop quickly in the beginning, they will soon hit a slump once they are caught up (or nearly caught up) to the established country in repeatable actions. Here, the country will begin to struggle. Their struggle will not likely be in their inability to play, but an inability to truly compete as a challenger. Why? Because the country has not yet established any competitive advantage, any uniquely better aspects, or any opportunities for ownership. The team will be great at imitation but not innovation.

Economic convergence theory validates that imitation is sufficient to "keep up" but not to "get ahead." Teams can follow the industry standard, follow the crowd, and follow competitors, and be okay enough to play the game but never be extraordinary enough to truly compete. This does not mean to disregard the lessons of others; it means to learn from others, draw inspiration from outside sources, and seek to improve and take ownership along the way.

How do we establish a competitive advantage?

Surely the answer is obvious by now. Effective collaborative ownership.

Why ownership?

If you do not take ownership, something or someone else will. Whether it be a process, tradition, method, policy, role, or project - take ownership. It is up to you to make your life, your organization, your world uniquely better than before.

Why collaboration?

If you can achieve your dreams all by yourself, you are not dreaming big enough. If you want to do something bigger than yourself, then you must include more than yourself.

Be empowered to make bold decisions on your own, be equipped to make bold decisions with others, and be confident to lead others in making bold decisions towards a connected vision. Seize opportunities for ownership and apply them in a way that no one else can for a true competitive edge.

Our academy teams had unique ownership in our processes of ball movement, methods of kicking the ball and communication, our projects of training and competing, our roles in the team, and projects on the pitch that gave us a competitive advantage over the rest. We collaborated using inspiration to cross-train in different areas, self-organized to lead training better, and worked together in synergy to cultivate a team that was more effective in playing the game.

I heard a story of an executive who, when discussing how to compete with Amazon in e-commerce, stated plainly, "We can't out Amazon, Amazon."

The executive illustrates a lesson for all. We can learn and take note of the strides from competitors. We can adapt and adjust, but at the end of the day, we cannot be a better version of someone else. We can only be the best version of ourselves.

Indian football will never win championships by trying to be a better version of French, American, English, Dutch, Brazilian, Argentinian, or Portuguese football. Indian football can learn from countries with more established football teams and take lessons and inspiration to build a foundation for sports, but Indian football will thrive by becoming the best *Indian* football team.

There is a contagious excitement and energy about the future of sport in India. Indian sports have the potential to be massive. While still an incipient movement, the world's second largest country is catching up quickly to be able to compete on the pitch. It's so thrilling to watch this remarkable country rise in the competition.

Your organization could copy the exact format as other established organizations. That is definitely a possibility. But after you get caught up, what is going to distinguish you from the rest? Learn from other organizations, but also find your competitive advantage within your opportunities for ownership in order to be uniquely better. Ask the questions:

- How can we be uniquely better and take ownership in our processes?
- How can we be uniquely better and take ownership in our methods?
- How can we be uniquely better and take ownership in our projects?
- How can we be uniquely better and take ownership in our roles?
- How can we be uniquely better and take ownership in our collaboration?
- How can we be uniquely better and take ownership in our captainship?

I coached a young lad named Achintiya who was six years of age. On his very first day of football, he came running onto the field and began shouting, "PASS!!! PASS!! PASS!!!" I noticed that Achintiya was yelling pass even when the other team had the ball. He was yelling pass when he was miles away from the action. He was yelling pass when he had the ball, so he was running with the ball shouting, "PASS! PASS! PASS!!!" I looked at Achintiya and I asked him, "Why are you yelling pass?" He looked up at me and said, "MissAmberMam, I do not know what it means. I only know that it is a football word."

Sometimes, I hear organizations sound a little bit like my friend Achintiya yelling, "Leadership! Teamwork! Creativity! Collaboration! Vision! Goals! Culture!" because we know that these are really good words that can lead to big wins, but if we are in the wrong position, if we are miles away from the action, or even if we have the ball and we do not know in which direction we are going, then these words are not only ineffective, but they are actually detrimental to the overall communication in the team. Eventually, the team will tune you out the way that my players tuned out Achintiya.

But if we take the time to build relationships and cast a clear vision, create a culture of creativity through opportunities for ownership in processes, methods, projects, and roles and if we build a culture of connected collaboration that refocusses from the scorecard to the scoreboard, and if we build a culture of captainship that defines, equips, and nurtures team leaders, then we will be in a position to yell pass, to receive the ball, to move forward, and to score really big goals.

Epilogue

As I was riding back to the Kempegowda International airport with Gongilal for the last time, I looked at the traffic wondering when I would return in person, recognizing that a part of my heart would never leave. Right before I departed, our teams had competed in a tournament. I watched as our players kicked the ball with confidence and then began to run without hesitation or glancing towards the sideline. Our players were focused on the goal. I watched as our players communicated with their team members, took ownership of their goals, and focused on the scoreboard rather than individual scorecards. I watched the scoreboard reflect the performance improvement on the pitch.

On my last day, I was completely humbled as I was showered with gifts and pictures, hugs, thanks, and tears. Silla, the player that brought her female family members to see me one day, gave me a beautiful large cross-over bag that was red, white, and blue. "MissAmberMam, it's the colors of your country but it's made in my country. It's like the two of us are woven together." This was a tough goodbye.

As I reflected on this journey, Gongilal began playing one last song on the radio, "Cham Cham." The lyrics read, "Cham cham cham, Main nachun aaj." This is translated as "I want to dance today." I smiled. India had given me plenty of reasons to dance and filled my heart with joy. G stopped at a food stall and I picked up my last masala dosa, and learned of yet another new spice included in this meal. The learning curve continued upward until my very last moments. When we arrived at the airport, I thanked G for everything, picked up my one backpack and suitcase, turned around, and left for the United States.

I share emails, social media, and even letters with some of my former players, and love seeing those who have decided to continue chasing their dreams of football and others that have decided to chase other dreams. Silla messages me sporadically with images of her dream board, videos of her practicing her football skills, and messages of updates with her life. She has a dream to be one of the first great female Indian footballers. She has an undying passion for the beautiful game. I believe that she is one to inspire the next generation of Indian athletes.

I believe that India has the potential to be a great sports nation. People like Silla, Praketh, Tejas, Benedict and Shreya are all over India and have the ability to inspire a generation the same way that they inspired me. They have the power to develop Indian sports to be uniquely better. I believe that all it takes is a dream, a step of faith, a little bit of luck, and effective, authentic, true collaborative ownership.

Works Cited

Bezos, Jeff. "A Conversation with Jeff Bezos." George W. Bush Presidential Center's Forum on Leadership in partnership with SMU. Forum on Leadership , 20 Apr. 2018, University Park, Texas , George W. Bush Presidential Center.

DeLong, Thomas, and Vineeta Vijayaraghavan. "Let's Hear It for B Players." *Harvard Business Review*. HBR Magazine, June 2003. Web. 17 Jan. 2021

"Learn About Volkswagen Violations." *EPA*, Environmental Protection Agency, www.epa.gov/vw/learn-about-volkswagen-violations.

Fox, Catherine Toth, et al. "At Whole Foods, the Team Votes You on or Off." *Hawaii Business Magazine*, 22 Apr. 2015, www.hawaiibusiness.com/at-whole-foods-the-team-votes-you-on-or-off/.

FIFA, www.fifa.com/tournaments/mens/worldcup/2014brazil.

Hancock, John Lee, director. *The Founder* . *IMDb*, The Weinstein Company, 2016, www.imdb.com/title/tt4276820/.

Krush, Alesia. "5 Success Stories That Will Make You Believe in Scaled Agile." *ObjectStyle*. 13 Jan. 2018. Web. 06 Jan. 2022.

Moon, Youngme, Mihir Desai, and Ryan Buell. "How Bad Is Airline Service, Really? And Other Customer Service Complaints." *After Hours Podcast*. Harvard Business Review - Afterhours Podcast, 31 Oct. 2018. Web. 12 Jan. 2021.

"NFL Player Alex Collins Says Irish Dance Is the Secret to His Football Success." CBS News, https://www.cbsnews.com/news/alex-collins-says-irish-dance-secret-football-success-nfl/, 24 Oct. 2017.

Pickett, Joe, director. *Space Jam*. Warner Brothers, 1996.

Stanley, Andy. "November 2017: Uniquely Better, Part 1." *Andy Stanley*. Andystanley.com, 04 Dec. 2019. Web. 17 Jan. 2021.

Stanley, Andy [@AndyStanley]. "Leaders who refuse to listen will eventually be surrounded by people who have nothing significant to say." Twitter, August 17, 2011, https://twitter.com/AndyStanley/status/103841035108630528.

CPSIA information can be obtained
at www.ICGtesting.com
Printed in the USA
JSHW051440130322
23659JS00006B/6